THE Pickleball Handbook

DAWN DAIS
Illustrations by Tim Alexander

THE Pickleball Handbook

An Unofficial Field Guide for Picklers Who Can't Stop, Won't Stop, and Probably Just Pulled a Muscle

CONTENTS

1

INTRODUCTION

Welcome to the Pickledome

Many people have tried to nail down what exactly pickleball is. Some say it's tiny tennis; others say it's oversized ping-pong. In reality, the best way to get an adequate understanding of the pickleball vibe is to picture a mixed martial arts octagon. But instead of burly fighters squaring off, imagine an intense face-off between a TikTok teenager in sneakers and a retiree donning a headband, scowl, and knee brace. One is fueled by youthful swagger, the other by decades of steely determination. And they are brawling in a sport where either one could feasibly come out utterly humiliated. This is the intensity you should be picturing when thinking of pickleball. Think passion. Think bloody rivalry. Think everyone from octogenarians to preteens with an insatiable hunger for victory.

Pickleball is not just a sport; it's a battlefield where friendships are forged and destroyed in the span of a single set. It's where mild-mannered accountants transform into paddle-wielding

PICKLEBALL
PRO SERIES
3 V 5
GO GRANDPA!

warriors, and bunco-playing grandmothers develop an unnerving killer instinct. It's where middle schoolers drop-shot their gym teachers into oblivion, and college athletes learn the hard way that pickleball skill is not determined by age. It's where newbies go from skeptics to full-blown addicts before they've even figured out how to properly announce the score; where the already competitive become even more insufferable. And where everyone—at some point—experiences the deep, personal betrayal of watching a perforated plastic ball sail past them, perfectly placed by an opponent they foolishly underestimated.

Because pickleball is much more than just a game—it's a cultural movement that defies age, fitness ability, and any level of common sense.

Sure, this description might seem a bit dramatic for a sport that features a modified wiffle ball, but underestimating pickleball is a rookie mistake. This "simple" sport often starts as a casual pastime and then quickly escalates into a full-blown obsession. One minute, you're innocently rallying with a friend, feeling smug about your hand-eye coordination; the next, you have flung yourself fully horizontal, leaping through the air, executing a dive you have no business attempting, all in the name of hitting that blasted plastic ball before it bounces on the ground. (The bloody part of pickleball can come about 3.5 seconds after gravity makes an appearance in your dive attempt.)

Not long after "casually" taking up pickleball, you will find yourself shouting things like "LET IT BOUNCE!" with the intensity of someone trying to defuse a bomb. The stakes? Irrationally high. The reward? Not much besides bragging rights, maybe a cheap plastic medal from a local tournament, and an occasional visit to your friendly neighborhood urgent care. Yet here we are—risking our dignity, our joints, and our weekend plans, all to chase the dink dream.

This is pickleball. And this is serious.

Why This Book Exists (And Why You Need It)

The Pickleball Handbook is your ultimate guide to surviving and thriving in the world's fastest growing obsession. Whether you're a pickleball newbie who got ambushed by an overly enthusiastic friend or a seasoned player who has more than one custom game shirt, this book is for you.

We'll cover:

- **The rules, which are both overly complicated and oddly arbitrary.**
- **The essential (and often unnecessary) gear you need to fit in.**
- **The many, many types of pickleball players, including Professor Paddle, the "Rusty" Ringer, and the person who is mostly here for selfies and social hour. (We will also touch on all the ways these many types of players will humble you along your pickleball journey.)**
- **The secret language of pickleball, from "dink" to "Nasty Nelson."**
- **How to know when you've crossed over from casual player to full-blown addict. (Hint: If you own a custom paddle, it's too late.)**

This book is here to both educate and entertain. If you're looking for a straightforward, deeply serious manual on the perfect pickleball technique, you may be in the wrong place. But if you want to understand the glorious absurdity of a sport that has somehow become the defining activity of a generation, then grab your paddle and let's get started. Maybe also grab a knee brace or two, just to be safe.

IS PICKLEBALL RIGHT FOR YOU?

A Very Scientific Quiz

Answer the following questions honestly. Your pickleball future depends on it.

1. **Do you enjoy activities that are technically low-impact but still somehow lead to countless new injuries?**
   A) Absolutely, full range of movement is overrated.
   B) No thanks, I prefer to remain in one fully functional piece.
2. **Are you prepared to take a sport played with a plastic ball way too seriously?**
   A) Yes, I think I'd look fantastic in pickleball goggles.
   B) No, I'm just here for a good time and possibly snacks.
3. **How many cuss words are you able to string together in a pinch?**
   A) My abilities are limitless.
   B) I'm too classy for such things.
4. **Are you comfortable with the possibility of being utterly humbled on the court by absolutely every demographic? We are talking all ages, body types, and skill levels. You are safe from no one.**
   A) Yes, and I will embrace my role as the athletic inferior to all other humans in existence.
   B) No, I have too much pride to lose to everyone.
5. **I hate to harp on this, but do you have health insurance?**
   A) Yes, and I'm fully prepared for whatever pickleball throws at me (including the ground).
   B) No, and I prefer to live on the edge—both physically and financially.

Mostly A's: Welcome to your new addiction. Pickleball isn't just a hobby for you—it's a lifestyle. Your weekends, your wardrobe, and possibly your retirement plans are now fully dedicated to the sport.

Mostly B's: You may not be convinced now, but pickleball has a way of sneaking into your life. One casual game turns into two, and before you can say "skinny singles," you find yourself stuck in an endless rabbit hole of YouTube pickleball tutorials at two A.M. It's only a matter of time—resistance is futile. But seriously: Make sure you have health insurance.

1

PICKLEBALL 101

How We Got Here and Where We Are

Pickleball, like so many confusingly popular things (goat yoga, mullets, *The Masked Singer*), was never really meant to get this big.

It was born in 1965, when some dads in Washington state (Joel Pritchard, Bill Bell, and Barney McCallum) tried to come up with a way to occupy their bored kids during summer break. They grabbed a wiffle ball, headed to the badminton court, and threw some old ping-pong paddles at the children. Their intention was to distract their offspring with physical activity for a few minutes, but instead they ended up creating a cultural phenomenon. (I personally have high hopes that "couch cushion fort building" will also become a professional sport soon, because I really dominated that skill during my own childhood summers.)

The origin of the name Pickleball is part of the sport's lore. Some say the game was named after the Pritchards' family dog, Pickles. But Joan Pritchard, Joel's wife, has said that she came up with the name because it reminded her of a pickle boat in crew races. That boat is made up of leftover or less experienced rowers who are seen as a group of misfits. This felt like a natural name to Joan, because pickleball seemed to be compiled from spare parts of so many other sports.

Misfits or not, what started as a way to kill a summer afternoon slowly mutated into a nationwide obsession—like sourdough bread, but with hamstring injuries. The sport gained traction in the Pacific Northwest, starting with friends and neighbors of Joel, Bill, and Barney. It turns out that a game meant to amuse children also did the trick for easily entertained adults.

By 1972, the game became legit, with the formation of Pickleball, Inc. (because nothing screams "chill backyard pastime" like legal paperwork). The corporation was created with the intent of protecting the sport and also, of course, monetizing it. Pickleball, Inc., began producing paddles, balls, and net systems, which helped the game grow beyond the Pacific Northwest. By 1984, the first official rulebook was published, and the USA Pickleball Association (USAPA) was founded soon after to promote the sport nationally.

From there, things escalated. By 1990, pickleball was being played in all fifty states, with courts popping up in schools, parks, and retirement communities. Retirees were early fans of the sport because it was easy to learn, low-impact, and just competitive enough to raise the heart rate above that found in a canasta tournament.

Then came the 2010s, and with them, younger players, legit tournaments, paddle tech innovation, and, most important, media coverage. Just when the sport seemed it might level out, COVID hit. Pandemic times required safe, social, outdoor activities, and pickleball was ready to meet the moment.

By 2023, the sport wasn't just a thing retirees did between water aerobics and bingo. It was everywhere: TikTok, the local news, and Sheila from accounting were all talking about this new craze. No one was safe from the spread of the Next Great Obsession.

And now here you are, reading a book that lovingly makes fun of pickleball, which is how you know the sport has officially reached the zeitgeist. Mockery, after all, is the highest form of flattery, especially when the one mocking is also one of the sport's biggest fans.

Before we get into the layout of the sacred pickleball court, let's talk about what you are actually supposed to do on one.

How to Pickle: The Short Version

The goal of this game is to hit the ball over the net and onto your opponent's side without breaking any rules, face-planting, or crying. (Aiming for two out of three is a good beginner goal.) You can play singles (one vs. one) or doubles (two vs. two), though doubles is more common, because everyone likes having someone else to blame if they lose. Pickleball is played using paddles that look like something between a racquetball racquet and a charcuterie board, and a modified wiffle ball that seems harmless, but is here to destroy everyone in its path.

Only the serving team can score; games are played to eleven points and must be won by two. Serves must be underhand, hit below the waist, and land diagonally into the opponent's service box. If the serve lands out of bounds or in the no-volley zone (more on that later), it's a fault (no good), but if it clips the net and still lands in the right spot, it's fair game (go team). (For more on the rules, see pages 17–30.)

After the serve, both sides must let the ball bounce once (the double bounce rule; see page 20) before anyone can volley (hit the ball out of the air, without it bouncing first). After that, it's a mix of hard hits, soft dinks (light hits), and the occasional rage smash (BLAM-O).

The game is played on what appears to be a shrunken-down tennis court (because it is often found drawn on pre-existing tennis courts) but is actually the size of a doubles badminton court. This is because badminton was the court used when the sport was being created for bored children all those years ago. It features a net that is about the same height as a tennis net, because said children had more fun hitting the ball over a net that was lower than the standard badminton height. There are some lines added to the court, and those lines are responsible for 87% of in-game arguments. There is also something called "the kitchen," which unfortunately has nothing to do with food and everything to do with gravity's cruel control over the human body.

To really understand how pickleball is played, you must understand its players. For a game that was invented to distract young children, it has done quite a number on adults as well. Over the years, pickleball has evolved into a strangely addictive hybrid of sport and social experiment. The energy coming off the players can run the gamut between friendly game night and Hulk Hogan ripping his shirt off in a ring circa 1985. And sometimes that energy can run the gamut through one player, during one game. More than rules or strategy or teamwork, energy is the biggest determinant of what happens on the pickleball court.

It all looks innocent enough . . . until you're sweating, swearing, and swatting at a plastic ball with less athleticism than should legally be allowed near anything labeled a sport. And that look? It's the unofficial look of pickleball: half desperation, half determination, and entirely more complicated than it has any right to be.

The Highly Official Pickleball Court Diagram

1. **Excuses Preparation Zone** Where players rehearse why they missed that last shot: "The sun was in my eyes," "Mercury is in retrograde," etc.

2. **Stretch It Out Spot** A great place to implement a quick thirty-two-point stretching regimen, just to loosen up the joints for continued battle, before each serve.

3. **Whisper Pep Talk Spot** Where to turn your back to the game before your serve and hype yourself up like a prizefighter between rounds.

4. **Ego Adjustment Area** Where you get up close and personal with your own athletic limitations.

5. **Foot Fault Free-For-All** No one knows the rules. Everyone thinks they do.

6. **Gravity's Playground** The area where you really want your dinks to land and really hope your face doesn't end up. Gravity is a cruel mistress, one with her own plans about who and what will land in this zone.

7. **Snack Zone** If you are lucky, this is like a line of food trucks, some offering kale-based energy bars, some offering IPAs. Befriend accordingly.

8. **Blame Bench** "I'm not saying it was all your fault, but . . . I have some notes."

9. **Side-Eye Section** Think gymnastics judges, but with less training and way more shade.

10. **Territory Dispute Line** "Yours!" said by both partners simultaneously, as the ball whizzes by.

11. **Cry Zone** Usually occupied after a difficult loss or an unfortunate run-in with an errant paddle.

12. **Best Group Selfie Spot** Great lighting, great background – if there aren't pictures, did it even happen?

13. **Insincere Paddle Tap Zone** What is said: "Good game." What is felt: "It's taking everything in my power to refrain from storming off like an angry toddler right now."

14. **Weird Flirty Energy Linger Zone** Where two players who just met already have a vibe.

15. **Where Lost Balls Go to Die** These balls flew too close to the sun. Or, rather, too far away for anyone to bother chasing them down. May their memory be eternal.

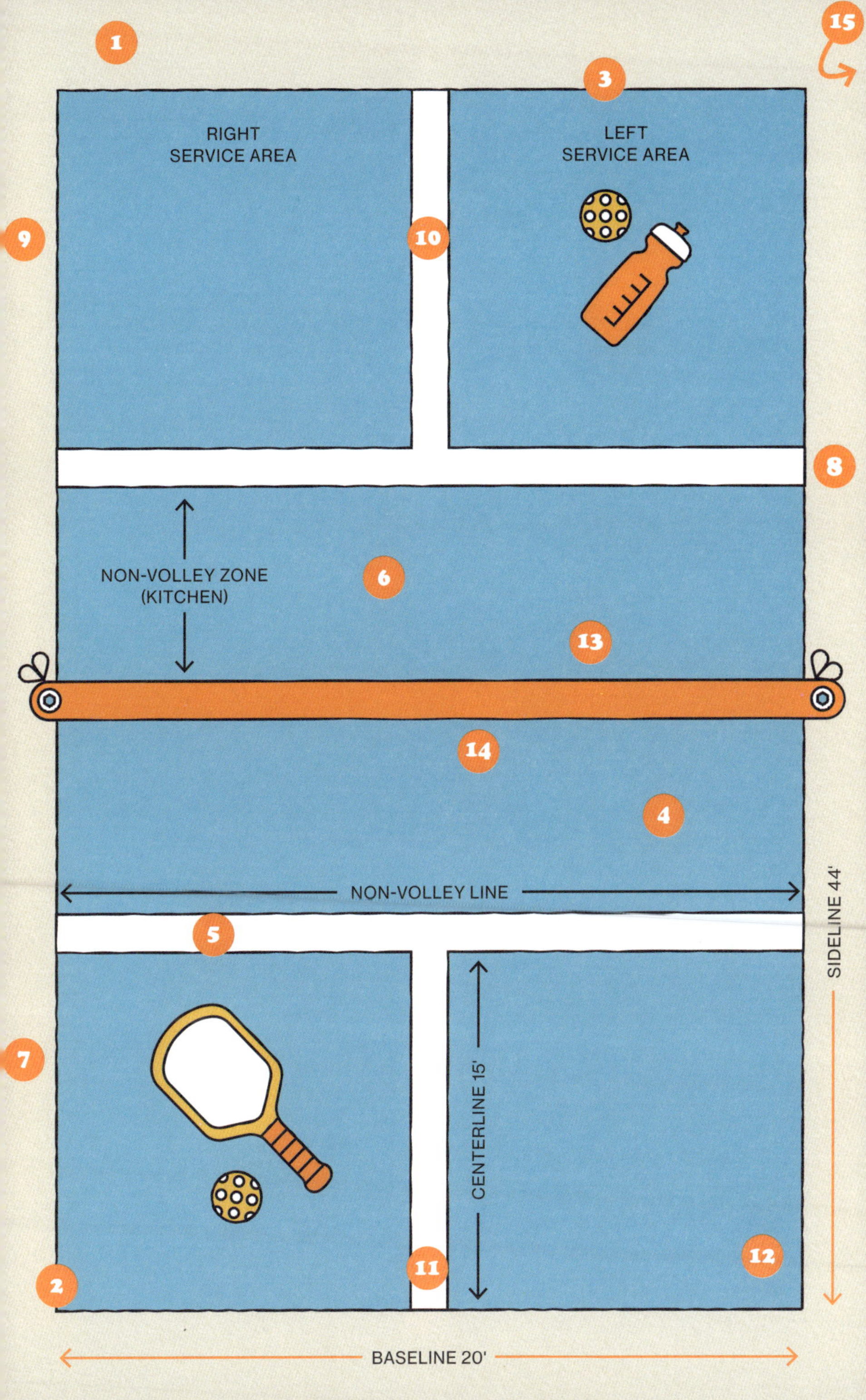
1
15
3
RIGHT
SERVICE AREA
LEFT
SERVICE AREA
9
10
8
NON-VOLLEY ZONE
(KITCHEN)
6
13
14
4
NON-VOLLEY LINE
5
SIDELINE 44'
7
CENTERLINE 15'
2
11
12
BASELINE 20'

Where to Pickle: The Court Where Sanity Goes to Die

When one first spots a pickleball court in the distance, the scene can look simple—quaint, even. People of all ages, tapping a ball back and forth over a net in a whimsical rhythm. Even as an unsuspecting onlooker gets closer, things continue to appear innocent enough. A tidy little rectangle, some cheerful lines, a net.

But something happens once a person steps inside those sidelines. Suddenly this is not just a court—this is a battlefield littered with sweatbands, knee braces, and the shattered egos of those who underestimated this "simple" sport.

The pickleball court is where rational human behavior is replaced by absurd competitiveness and unfortunate fashion. Where grown adults risk it all for a plastic ball that is far beyond their reach ("all" being their ligaments), become way too confident in their aging eyesight ("That ball was IN!"), and treat casual recreational play like Game Seven of the World Series (sometimes they also hit the ball so far out of bounds, it appears as if they are actually playing baseball).

The drama of the pickleball court will rival anything you've ever seen on Bravo and will ultimately be more confusing as well. Why do these little courts produce such strong emotions? Why are people so drawn to the call of compulsive competitiveness? What the hell is a kitchen, and why is it a part of any legitimate sport?

Come along with me as I break down the sacred geography of the court—every line, zone, and hotspot where chaos is known to flourish. We'll break down the technical terms (like "kitchen") and translate them into what they really mean (Gravity's Playground).

We'll also introduce *enhanced* features not sanctioned by any official rulebook—like the Snack Corner, the Cry Zone, and the highly competitive Best Group Selfie Spot.

Because here's the thing: Pickleball isn't just a game. It's a lifestyle. It's cardio with consequences. A questionably officiated drama performed with paddles. And it all begins on this deceptively cheerful little slab of madness.

Let's hit the court. Bring your paddle, your pride, and a prayer or two.

Now you know where pickleball came from, the gist of how to play it, and the many emotional danger zones lurking on the court. Next up: the rules. Because yes, pickleball is 83% cheerful chaos and 15% muscle pulls, but that last 2% is the rulebook that holds this patchwork sport together.

2

THE RULES, OR LACK THEREOF

A Sport Held Together by Vibes, Loose Interpretations, and That One Guy Who Printed Up a Laminated Rulebook for Handy Referencing

The rules of pickleball were invented on the fly, an improvised mix of logic and whoever yelled their idea the loudest. Like any great backyard game, the rules evolved through the time-honored strategy of "no ideas are bad ideas . . . but *my* ideas are the best ideas." The result? A rulebook with the structural integrity of a very wobbly Jenga tower.

Now, decades later, pickleball has grown into a billion-dollar industry with pro tours, televised tournaments, and a rabid fan base. But even with all that, pickleball still has the vibe of a backyard game invented by three dudes after splitting a twelve-pack. That is one reason the sport is so appealing, but it's also why the rules can be so confusing.

The official pickleball rulebook seems to be a living document, one that changes as the sport matures and depends on where it is being played. Some people swear by traditional scoring. Others insist rally scoring is "the future." Some call foot faults as if they are at Wimbledon, while others don't mind if you hopscotch through the kitchen.

Even the professionals can't seem to agree. Rule changes are constant, debates litter the interwebs, and just when you think you've got it figured out, someone will say, "But I heard about this new rule on a podcast the other day . . ."

So, as you step onto the court, just remember: This all started as a backyard free-for-all designed to wear kids out. You have been trained by years of Red Rover, The Floor Is Lava, and dodgeball. You were built for this level of mildly structured nonsense, and your time has come to shine.

The Serve: The Overthought Underhand

Let's get started; this should be simple enough. A little serve over the net to commence the pickling. Just hit the ball *underhand, below your waist,* with an *upward motion.* Simple, right?

Spoiler: Nothing about this is simple.

First, let's talk about the "underhand" requirement. Apparently, that definition is open to wildly varying interpretations. Some players go under, some players come from the side, and others look as though they are swatting at a pesky mosquito. Approximately seven out of ten serves inspire a whisper from the other team, "Was that even legal?"

Then comes the waist debate. Whose waist? Jeff, who's 6'4", or Carol, who's 5'1"? Because those are very different strike zones.

But wait, there's more. The "drop serve" was introduced to simplify serving. But, I hate to break it to you, it's not simple. Players can drop the ball (a simple drop, with no toss or bounce added) and allow it to bounce before hitting it. But from how high can they drop it? Can they spin it at all? Can they stare directly into their opponent's eyes as they drop, like it's personal?

Before long, you've got four players locked in a heated rules debate, one person googling USA Pickleball's website on their phone, and at least one exasperated player declaring, "Just serve however you want!"

Congratulations: You haven't even hit the ball yet, and no one can agree on how this game is actually played.

SERVING WITH STYLE

While the rulebook lays out the mechanics of serving, it says nothing about the flair. Spend five minutes at your local court and you'll witness many

The Fastball Fantasy

This server winds up as if they are about to throw a major league fastball . . . only to finish the serve by tapping the ball with the force of a delicate golf putt.

The Bounceinator

They bounce the ball no fewer than 4,387 times before every serve, as though they're building dramatic tension for a series finale. By the time they actually hit it, you've aged five years and completely forgotten the score of this game.

players who are deeply invested in razzle-dazzle, with their serve being their primary method of dazzling. From athletic overkill to interpretive dance energy, here are a few serving styles you're likely to witness (or maybe accidentally invent).

The Bowling League

This server is calling on their other recreational pastime, with a serve that finishes with a dramatic bowler's follow-through. No guarantee where the ball will end up, but the swagger is undeniable.

The Telenovela Betrayal

This serve features another dramatic windup, but instead feels like the kind you'd expect right before someone gets slapped across the face in a soap opera love triangle. Then ***WHACK!*** That ball takes the hit as if it just ran off with your sibling and stole your inheritance.

The Double Bounce Rule: The Great Confusion

On paper, this rule sounds easy enough: After the serve, the ball must bounce once on each side before anyone can hit it out of the air (volley). That's it. That's the rule. It was designed to slow the game down and keep things fair.

What it actually does is inspire frantic "Let it BOUNCE!" cries from newbies and instant regret from veterans who have a brain glitch and forget the rule. It also results in an emotional roller coaster every time a player makes *the best return shot ever,* only to realize they *forgot to let the blasted ball bounce*.

After a few bounce-related mishaps, players tend to lock up like a malfunctioning Roomba—standing motionless, eyes wide, waiting for their partner to make the first move and whispering, "I have no idea if it needs to bounce."

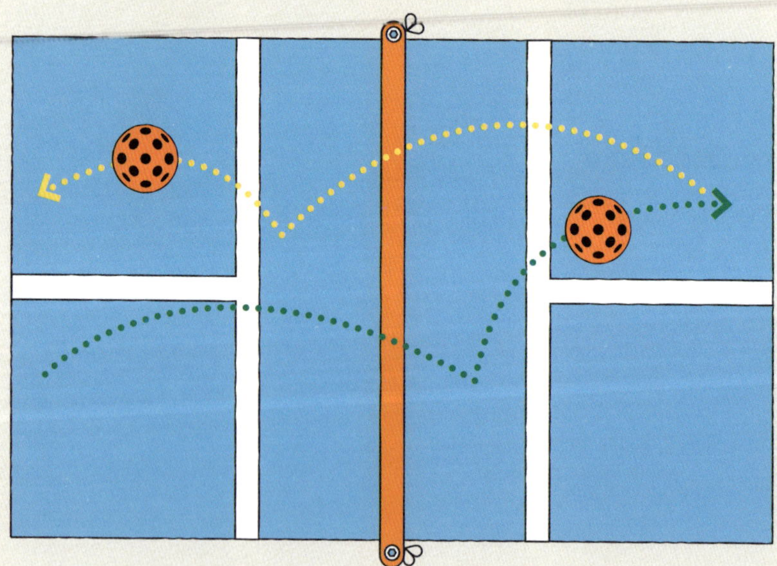

The Let Serve Confusion

Back in the day, pickleball had a rule called the "let serve." If a serve touched the top of the net but landed in the right box, the serve was replayed. Then, in a stunning plot twist, the let serve rule was removed entirely. Now, if a serve lands in the correct service box, whether it hits the net or not, the ball is live—play on.

Unfortunately, not everyone has received the memo about this rule change, and a general wave of confusion blankets the court every time a serve hits the net. (Just one more layer on top of the already overstuffed comforter set of pickleball chaos.)

In short, the *actual* rule is: no more lets. But if you want to keep friends, maybe just replay it anyway.

The Kitchen: Gravity's Playground

Officially called the "non-volley zone," the kitchen is a seven-by-twenty-foot rectangle on each side of the net, stretching the full width of the court and extending seven feet back from the net. The rule regarding the non-volley zone is that, you guessed it, there are no volleys allowed while standing in, stepping into, or pirouetting through the kitchen. Even if a toe is just grazing the kitchen line while a player is volleying, it is considered a fault, and the player loses the point.

On the other hand, a player can set up permanent residence in the kitchen and hit as many balls as they want to, as long as those balls have bounced before they are hit.

It sounds straightforward. It is not.

The second someone mentions "kitchen violation," the courtroom drama begins.

"What if just my paddle crosses the line?"

"What if I hit the ball, then fall into the kitchen after a valiant ten-second battle against inertia?"

"What if my shoelace is touching the line, but I'm not emotionally present anywhere in the vicinity?"

Let's be clear–stepping on the line is the same as stepping in the kitchen. Falling into the kitchen after the ball is hit? Also a fault. Running up to the net and slamming a volley into the esophagus of your opponent while standing in the kitchen? You need anger management counseling.

Kitchen violations are the classic rookie move, and how strictly they're called usually depends on the group's mood–ranging from "blatant ignoring" to "public shaming."

Either way, gravity always wins.

Stay out of the kitchen. It's a recipe for disaster.

Scoring: Just Yell Out Some Numbers with Confidence and See What Happens

Scoring in pickleball seems straightforward until you realize you have to say *three* numbers before every serve, and that is apparently one too many numbers for most newbie brains to fully comprehend.

The whole thing feels an awful lot like being called on in math class, and it inspires an equal number of blank stares throughout the game. Add in rally scoring (used in some leagues and tournaments), and suddenly the only thing anyone agrees on is that they have no idea what's happening.

Scoring is announced like this:

1. Your team's score.
2. The opponent's score.
3. Whether you're the first or second server (since both partners serve once each possession, except for the first serve, when only one partner serves . . . because why not?).
4. So if your team is winning 7 to 3 and you are the second person to serve on your side, you'll announce, "Seven, three, two" before serving. If you are a beginner, you will probably also add in, "Right?" because it will be a long time before you are fully confident in your score-calling abilities.

Scoring, Again: Side-Out vs. Rally

In pickleball, the difference between side-out scoring and rally scoring is basically the difference between a polite dinner party and a food fight. In side-out scoring (the most common and widely used scoring technique), only the serving team can score points. So if your team wins a rally, but the other team is serving? No points for you. If you win the rally and the other team's first server is serving, then the serve just moves to their second server. You still don't get the ball back. But if the second server is serving and you win the rally? That's a side-out, and your team finally gets the serve, and the chance to win some points. It's a slower, more strategic system that rewards patience, precision, and people who don't mind earning their victories one sweaty point at a time.

Rally scoring, on the other hand, turns every rally into a potential point no matter who serves. This means the score moves faster, the game ends sooner, and everyone is in a constant state of panic at all times. It's great for those who enjoy instant gratification and/or watching their lead disappear in ninety seconds. It's mayhem with a scoring system, but it gets the job done.

THE "NO ONE KNOWS WHY . . ." RULES

- **Start with the second server.** In a doubles game, both players on the same team normally get a chance to serve until they lose a point. But on the very first serve of the game, the serving team only gets one server before the serve switches sides. Why? No one knows. Tradition? Vibes? Some say it balances the advantage of serving first, but it mostly just feels like an attempt to keep players confused from the jump.

- **On a serve, the ball can hit any line—except the kitchen line.** If the ball grazes a line on the diagonally opposite box during a serve, it's considered in . . . unless it touches the kitchen line. Why? Because consistency is overrated.

- **You can hit the ball around the post (yes, really).** If you can somehow hit the ball *around* the outside of the net post without touching the net, it's completely legal. Does it feel illegal? Absolutely. Does it look as if you've left the court and the sport entirely? Also yes. This rule seems as though it was invented when someone pulled off this move, paused for dramatic effect, and the pickleball community collectively decided, "Sure, why not?"

Line Calls: Where Sportsmanship Meets Side-Eye

In pickleball, the ball is considered in if any part of it touches the line, except during the serve. On a serve, the ball can bounce on any line around the box where you are serving and still be in . . . except the kitchen line. If it touches the kitchen line, even a teeny tiny bit, it's out.

During regular play, all lines are fair game, including the kitchen line, so if a ball grazes a sideline, baseline, or the kitchen line after the serve, it's still in.

Throughout the game, players make their own line calls. Usually whoever is closest to the ball makes the call, but anyone on the court (and usually people off the court as well) can chime in with their opinion. No refs, no replays, just good old-fashioned sportsmanship. Technically, you're supposed to give your opponent the benefit of the doubt. Realistically? Close calls usually test the limits of good old-fashioned sportsmanship.

Most players fall into one of two camps:

The Saint: "Eh, it was probably in. Your point."

The Sniper: "It was out. By a millimeter. I had the only angle that could properly see where it landed. My point."

What follows can either be the equivalent of a jovial group hang or reminiscent of an uncomfortable Thanksgiving dinner meltdown with your dysfunctional family. Tread lightly.

Embrace the Shrug

If you've made it this far, you might have noticed a pattern when it comes to the rules of pickleball. And that pattern is: "These are the rules . . . unless they aren't."

It's a good idea to go out onto the court with a general familiarity with the rules of pickleball, but it's a better idea to understand the universal truth of pickleball: Every court has its own rules, and those rules might change halfway through the game, depending on who's losing.

But here's the thing—no one really cares if you get all the rules perfect, and most players are open to a little flexibility in the name of good fun. Remember, we are playing a game that was stitched together on the fly by parents desperate to burn their kids' energy before bedtime. In many ways, we are all those children, running around, having fun on a warm summer night. We might not know exactly what we are doing, but we show up, paddles in hand, ready for another round of glorified recess disguised as recreation.

So what's the real rule?

Have fun, be fun, and try your best not to belly flop into the kitchen like it's a Slip 'N Slide.

THE ULTIMATE PICKLE PERSONALITY

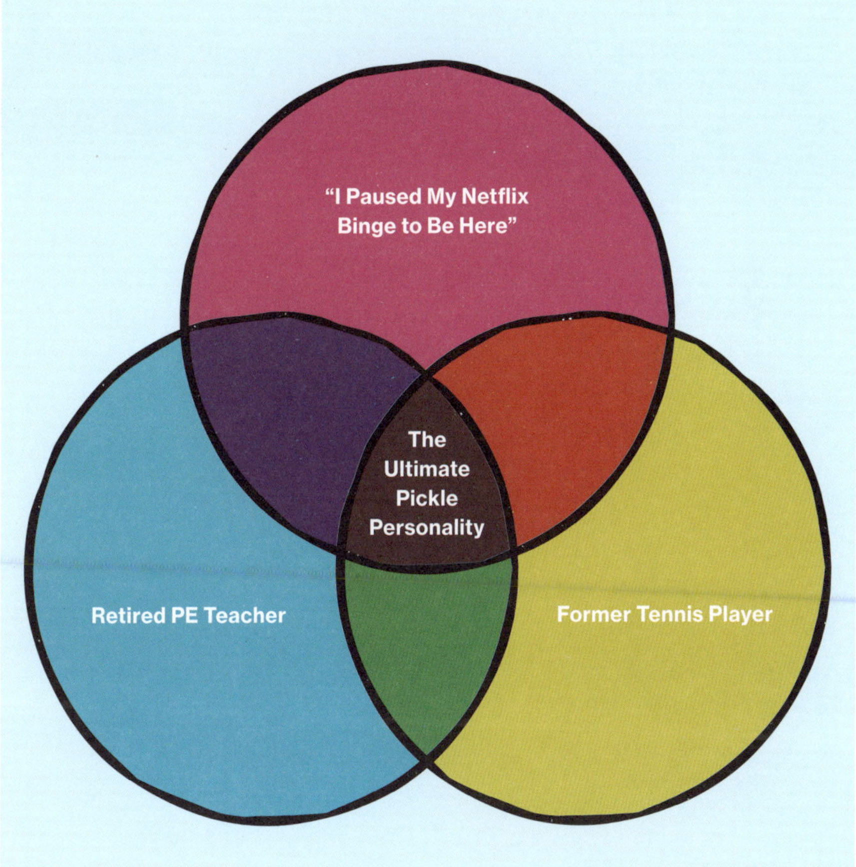

REGIONAL QUIRKS

If you travel to new courts, prepare to hear phrases like:

"Time-outs granted for spontaneous birdwatching."
—Portland

"If your hat falls off mid-point, we replay it—we respect the accessories."
—Los Angeles

"Tornado or heat stroke: only five-minute delay allowed"
—Amarillo

Pickleball rules change from court to court like dialects in a foreign country. Just smile, nod, and act like you're fluent.

3

HOW TO SPEAK PICKLEBALL

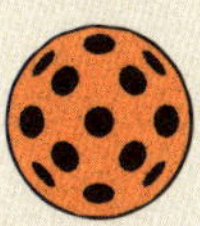

Decoding the Sport's Most Absurd Jargon

Like any proper subculture, pickleball is chock-full of vocabulary that makes zero sense. It has its own language made up of words that sound fake, feel ridiculous to say, and really make you question the sobriety of the people who created this sport. One minute you're trying to figure out which side to serve from, and the next you're attempting to navigate the linguistic circus that is pickleball.

But we all know that a pastime without ridiculous slang is not a pastime worth fully committing to. And learning to speak pickleball is not optional; it's a survival tactic. One cannot simply master the skills of pickleball; one must also master the language. (The good news is, silly slang is a lot easier to master than a reliable backhand, so you've got that going for you.) You don't just hit the ball—you dink it, drive it, or drop it. You don't just stand on the court—you stack, poach, and pivot. And if you lose 11–0? Well, you've just been pickled (a phrase that sounds like a lot of different things, none of them involving a wiffle ball).

What follows is some of the sport's most iconic, confusing, and wonderfully unnecessary jargon so that, at the very least, you can confidently nod along during a postgame wrap-up. I'll also sprinkle in some completely made-up words and phrases, because honestly, no one's likely to notice the difference as long as you say them with confidence.

Let's get started on this crash course in Pickleball Speak. Because if you can't master the shots, you might as well dominate the vocabulary.

Food-Themed Terms

Falafel A weak, dead shot with no power, usually followed by another F word from the player who hit it.

Flapjack A shot that must bounce before it's hit, either on the serve or return of the serve.

Kitchen The non-volley zone, located seven feet from the net on both sides.

Pickle The name of the game; no one really knows why.

Pickled Losing 11–0. Not a great look.

Pickler A person hopelessly addicted to pickleball.

Poach Jumping into your partner's territory for a shot.

Chili Cheese French Fries* An ill-advised lunge for a ball way beyond reach that seems like a good idea at the time, but almost immediately causes the player pain and regret.

Cauliflower* A player who is trying to do too much on the court, like cauliflower tries to do too much on menus throughout the land.

Ice Cream Truck* An errant ball that seems to roll on forever, forcing a player to bob and weave through other games while trying to run it down like a kid chasing an ice cream truck through the neighborhood.

Terms That Sound Very High Stakes

Drive Less "high-speed chase," more "muscle flex with questionable control," a drive is a hard, direct shot that says, "Welcome to the big leagues."

Stack Not a tactical military move, a stack is when partners line up on the same side of the court to start the point and then move to their pre-decided side post-serve (see page 127). It's used to optimize court positioning but can also optimize confusion.

Pivot Sounds like something yelled in a war room (or during an intense couch negotiation up a flight of stairs), but in pickleball, pivoting means rotating your body and feet (without lifting your anchor foot) to stay balanced and ready to handle any shot.

Foot Fault Feels as though it should be screamed during the finale of a courtroom drama: "Foot fault, your honor!" But it just means your foot has faulted into the kitchen during a volley shot. It's probably a decent idea to expect courtroom-level exasperation from your opponents, if you are playing against sticklers.

Paddle Identity* When a player shows up with a new paddle and, as a result, a completely different personality and play style. Are they in witness protection? Do they have amnesia? Will they add a roundhouse kick to the game? No one knows for sure.

Terms That Could Also Be Insults

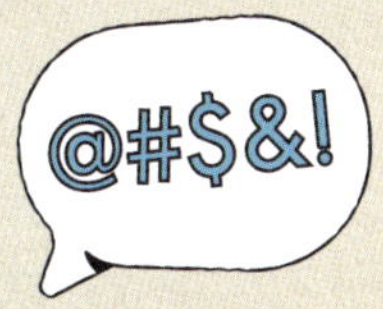

Dillball Though similar to one of my favorite insults, "douche nozzle," this actually describes a shot that is inbounds and has bounced once, a live ball.

Dink No, your intelligence is not being called into question; this describes a soft, controlled shot that just clears the net and drops into the kitchen.

Nasty Nelson Similar to a "wet willy" or a "wedgie," this is when a server intentionally hits the non-receiving opponent with the ball, resulting in a fault for the receiving team and a point for the serving team.

Opa! No, your mother isn't disappointed in you; this is shouted after the serve and return hits, when volleys are officially in play.

Paddle Face Sounds like a taunt from your little brother, but this refers to the material that is used to cover the surface of a paddle.

Kitchen Chicken* A player who will go nowhere near the kitchen, for fear they will unintentionally fault into it as though it is inescapable quicksand.

Lob Goblin* Someone who lives to lob every single ball, forcing their opponents to sprint backward for each hit like a toddler chasing a balloon.

Terms That Sound Like Band Names

ATP (Around the Post) Shot hit around the net post, or a 1980s rap group.

Banger A player who hits everything hard, or possibly a death metal band.

Third Shot Drop A soft, strategic third shot that is played after the serve and return and lands in the kitchen, allowing the serving team to move up to the net; also a 1990s emo band.

Tweener A shot made between the legs, or a Weezer cover band.

Unforced Error A mistake made on an easy shot when there was absolutely no excuse besides user error; also perhaps a teenage garage band.

Volley Llama Illegally volleying in the kitchen (the non-volley zone), or a Thursday-night headliner at the country bar down the street.

Ghost Paddle* When the ball somehow flies through your paddle, even though the paddle was clearly in the correct formation; also a DJ who performs only under black light at raves.

Kitchen Riot* When paddles are paddling and feet are faulting all over the kitchen during a dink rally; also a punk band that's overly committed to hairspray and eyeliner.

* These terms are not real . . . yet. Get out on the court and make them happen!

Muppet-Themed Terms

Erne A shot taken while jumping over the kitchen, with you landing just outside the sideline after slamming the ball back to the opposing team. Looks really cool when it is pulled off. Often results in a pulled hamstring either way. (Actually named after pro pickleball player Erne Perry.)

Bert This is just like an Erne, but it is a surprise cross-court poach where a player jumps in front of their partner to hit an Erne, while leaping through the air like a gazelle who has yet to learn about gravity.

Big Bird* A highly advanced formation where one partner leaps on the shoulders of the other, creating an unstoppable lobbing machine.

Oscar* Much like the Grouch himself, this player stays in one place the whole game, hurling trash talk.

Kermit* A jovial newbie who bumbles around the court hitting balls with abandon and enthusiasm.

So there you have it, your unofficial guide to speaking fluent pickleball. Will it help you win? Probably not. But it'll make you sound like you know what you're doing. Add some swagger and a finger gun or two, and you're golden.

4

FASHION ON THE COURT

From Sensible Sneakers to Neon Madness

There are many stages in the transformation from pickleball newbie to full-blown paddle junkie. These steps involve the gradual evolution of mind, body, skill, and swagger. The stages can be small or large, laborious or sudden. But no part of the pickleball metamorphosis is more visible, more dramatic, or more deeply unhinged than the player outfit.

Because nothing announces your progression quite like what you've decided to wear to a public court at nine A.M. on a Tuesday.

One minute you're in your faded Turkey Trot T-shirt and some worn-out sweatpants, silently judging the players who look as if they've popped out of the pages of *Pickle Power Weekly,* and the next, you're $327 deep into "pickleball-specific" attire, considering whether your compression sleeves clash with your UV-blocking visor. It's a slippery slope, and the slide is inevitable.

In most sports, fashion is about performance, convention, or avoiding injury. In pickleball? It's about letting everyone know exactly who you are *as a person* . . . via your skort and/or headband. It's less "athletic wear," more "synthetic zodiac sign."

There was a time when people approached the pickleball court as though they were headed to mow the lawn, wearing whatever was clean-ish, stretchy, and didn't smell *too bad.* Stained concert T-shirt from a band that broke up twenty years ago? Check. Elastic-waist shorts that were too tragic to even make it into the Goodwill pile? Yep. Running shoes that had never actually moved faster than a brisk walk? Perfect. That's how the pickle party started—relaxed, blissfully unpolished, and undeterred by societal expectations surrounding what qualifies as "acceptable for public display."

But then something changed.

T-Shirt Wall of Shame

- Dink Around and Find Out
- Kitchen Patrol
- Paddle Baddie
- Live Laugh Lob
- Will Dink 4 Drinks
- Straight Outta the Kitchen
- That's Nasty, Nelson

As with all things fun and low-stakes, humans couldn't leave pickleball alone. We took a chill backyard pastime and injected it with the competitive chaos of the Olympic trials. And once casual fun was escorted off the premises, Serious Athlete™ showed up. And Serious Athlete, of course, demanded a serious fit. Sure, the actual skill level hadn't quite caught up to the label of Serious Athlete, but like many greats who have greated through time, players knew well enough to fully embrace the time-honored tradition forged in the fires of mediocre talent: "Fake it till you make it." Or in this case, "Drop an irresponsible amount of money on flashy apparel to distract from your complete lack of skill . . . till you make it."

Because if you're going to miss the ball, you might as well look fantastic doing it.

Today, people no longer just throw on some random clothes and head out for a game with friends. Fashion has become the way to let those friends (and mostly strangers) know exactly what kind of pickleball player you are. Obnoxious pickle-themed shorts? Your playing style is unstoppable organized chaos. Color-coordinated paddle and tank? You place the ball just inside the line with the precision of a trained sniper. Personalized visor? The spin on your shots is the stuff of legends.

In fact, the progression of pickleball fashion in the world almost perfectly mirrors what happens to each individual player who enters the sport. So much so that a player's fashion choices have become a pretty decent way to determine where said player is on their journey to Pickle Passion.

Let's break down the pickleball progression now. Keep in mind that these steps have nothing to do with pickleball acumen and everything to do with pickleball obsession. There is Kool-Aid, and the more you drink, the deeper you spiral into the neon-lit rabbit hole of pickleball fashion that the internet is all too happy to offer.

Consider yourselves, and your bank account, warned.

PICKLEBALL FASHION CRIMES

STAGE 1
The Entry-Level Ensemble
(Aka the "I'm Probably Going to Drink Beer in the Parking Lot After This Game" Look)

Everyone starts here. You don't know the rules yet, you have no idea what a "dink" is, and you're definitely not investing real money into this activity that you're 92% sure you're only doing once.

You're wearing whatever is clean enough to not get you kicked off the court.

Typically:

- **A faded team-building T-shirt from a job you quit a decade ago**
- **Some "yoga" pants or "basketball" shorts that haven't seen a Downward Dog or a free throw line in quite some time**
- **Sneakers that you forgot you owned until twenty minutes before you left for the game**
- **And if you're feeling *fancy,* a trucker hat, to really demonstrate your commitment to fashion**

The vibe here is "I'm here to move, not impress anyone." You are not alone. This is where all great(ish) pickleballers begin. But you will not stay here.*

Because soon, you'll start to notice . . . things.

STAGE 2
The Awareness Phase*

You look around the court and realize that some people are taking this game *very* seriously.

They have coordinated outfits. Their paddles match their shoes. Their visors have SPF ratings (and they knew that was a thing). They are doing . . . stretches? Preemptive stretches. Who even are these people?

At first, you scoff. "It's just a game," you mutter while casually crossing your arms to obscure the "Namaste in Bed" graphic on your shirt. But something starts to shift inside you. Maybe it's envy. Maybe it's respect. Maybe it's the creeping realization that you look less like a proper player and more like a retiree who got separated from a cruise excursion and wandered onto a pickleball court.

So you buy real court shoes. And maybe a hat that doesn't double as your "lazy hair day" disguise. Nothing crazy. Just a few little items that let it be known, "I know how to properly announce the score before I serve."

Congratulatons. You are now visually invested. And the slope only gets slipperier from here.

* It is extremely rare, but occasionally a player remains at this stage permanently. These players are diabolical. They break the unspoken, sacred rule of pickleball: that we should all be able to determine our opponent's skill level from a quick once-over of their outfit. When a player saunters up to the court in a sun-bleached bucket hat and flip-flops, we expect confusion, not competence. But then they proceed to annihilate all adversaries with a completely unbothered demeanor? That's not a player. That's a problem. A mystery wrapped in mesh and mismatched socks. Respect them. Fear them. But do not underestimate them.

THE PICKLE PROGRESSION

Stage 1

The "I've Played a Lot of Ping-Pong!" Man

The Look: Faded Turkey Trot T-shirt, mismatched gym shorts that haven't ever been off the couch, tube socks with holes in them, $12 Target sneakers, mildly offensive trucker hat.

The "Can We Grab Apps After This?" Woman

The Look: Ex's oversized T-shirt, yoga pants so stretched they're basically honorary sweatpants, a pair of fashion sneakers that are designed more for emotional support than arch support.

Stage 2

The "I Might Like This Even More Than Ping-Pong" Man

The Look: Slightly newer T-shirt, real athletic shorts, ball cap (facing forward), basic court shoes, some socks without holes.

The "I Bet I Could Be Good at This" Woman

The Look: Slightly upgraded athletic capris and tank (bought on clearance "just to see"), a loaner paddle from a pickleball enthusiast, hair pulled back in a messy bun that means business, dusty cross-trainers.

THE PICKLE PROGRESSION

Stage 3

The "Weekend Warrior" Man

The Look: Branded dry-fit polo in a color that can be best described as aggressively teal, name-brand court shoes, wraparound sunglasses that might have been stolen from a Tour de France cyclist, one (just one) compression sleeve.

The "Coordinated and Competitive" Woman

The Look: A skort with a ball pocket, pickleball-specific shoes with a name like PicklePower Pro 7 (because clearly six versions just weren't *pro* enough), a performance pickleball visor (because apparently that's a thing).

. . . CONTINUED

Stage 4

The "Dink Daddy"

The Look: A custom dry-fit shirt with "Dink Daddy" splashed across the chest in varsity lettering, fingerless gloves (for "paddle control"), compression socks pulled up to his knees (to better display the pickleball pattern), a backup paddle that he refers to as "The Closer."

The "Paddle Princess"

The Look: A coordinated outfit and paddle combo that she describes as "kitchen couture," a sun visor that proudly declares "Dropshot Like It's Hot" in rhinestones, limited edition court shoes, a fully loaded smartwatch for tracking every drop of blood, sweat, and tears.

STAGE 3
The Weekend Warrior Makeover

Here's where the wardrobe decisions become . . . deliberate.

You're playing weekly now. Maybe even multiple times a week. You've joined a group chat with a name like "Dinks & Drinks," "The Paddle Posse," or something equally ridiculous. You are in it.

Your newbie outfit? Gone. Banished to the back of your closet, along with the illusion that this was ever going to be a casual hobby. You, my friend, are evolving. And your closet is evolving with you.

You've now replaced your rookie look with:

- **Performance tops made of fabric that promises to "breathe" (which is good, because you're still gasping for air after every rally)**
- **Neon. So much neon.**
- **Skorts or shorts with hidden ball pockets (because you are now a person who prioritizes ball storage options when choosing attire [totally normal stuff happening here])**
- **A paddle backpack with more storage compartments than you truly know what to do with (so you just fill them with snacks and delusion)**
- **Court shoes with technology that rivals a Sleep Number bed (featuring a similar price point as well)**

You've officially crossed into the realm of aesthetic commitment. You no longer just show up to play—you arrive dressed to handle business.

And this is only Stage 3. Buckle up. The slide gets weirder.

STAGE 4
The Fully Pickled

This is the final form. There's no turning back now.

Your closet looks a lot like your social media feed—heavy on pickleball, light on reality. And that ratio makes sense, because most of your closet items have been purchased from extremely accurate, slightly judgmental ads targeted at "easily influenced pickleballers who are making poor budgeting decisions at two A.M."

You've clicked "Add to Cart" more times than you've successfully executed a third shot drop, and you have zero regrets.

At this stage, you don't just play the game; you *dress like it's your job.* And honestly, it would work out much better if it were your job, because then you'd have a lot more things to wear to work.

Your look includes:

- **Matching paddle and paddle cover (this pretty much goes without saying at this point)**
- **Pickleball socks that are thick, moisture-wicking, and covered in ironic pickleball phrases and/or caricatures**
- **Paddle-themed earrings, bracelets, nail decals, or possibly a tattoo if you had too many celebratory drinks while in the vicinity of a tattoo parlor after last week's match**
- **A towel clipped to your waistband "just in case"**
- **Or, even better, pickleball attire that has two layers: a wick-away material next to your body and a towel-like fabric on the exterior, for you to wipe your hands on during the game (what a time to be alive!)**

- **A compression sleeve or knee brace that mutters "injury prevention" but screams "my doctor has already warned me that this sport is a bad idea"**
- **Performance sunglasses built with nine layers of lens technology to protect you from UV rays . . . and dignity, probably**

You now identify as a Serious Athlete™, which means your entire aura feels like a TED Talk titled "How to Overcommit to a Hobby." You pack your paddle on every trip, just in case. You now remember the names of pro pickleballers more easily than the names of your kids' teachers. And you might have considered starting a pickle podcast.

Welcome. You've made it. The pattern on your shorts is legally classified as a distraction, and that's the point.

NAKED PICKLEBALL

The Bare Essentials

When exploring the universe of pickleball fashion, it's important to include all styles: the bold, the bright, and the bare. Yes, "naked pickleball" is real, and surprisingly popular among people who reject society's quaint little rule about keeping your private parts . . . um, private. It's the ultimate minimalist look: no shoes, no visor, no wick-away fabric. Just a paddle, a blatant disregard for gravity, and an overwhelming amount of confidence (plus sunscreen, please). It says something about pickleball's reach that even the naturist community couldn't resist. If people dedicated to living against the grain (and against clothing) can't resist the pickleball pull, truly no one is safe.

BINGO!
Player makes sure to set their smartwatch to "pickleball" before the first serve
Neon from head to toe
A hat dramatically gets turned backward during a difficult game
Customized paddle cover
Crocs in sport mode
Fanny pack worn unironically
Shirt with pun
Custom Etsy-ordered skort/shorts

PICKLE GEAR

Sweatbands, Knee Braces, and Glory

Pickleball, by design, requires very little equipment: A paddle. A ball. Some decent shoes. A reasonably flat court. At least one other person to hit the ball back to you from the other side of the net. And that's about it. What a delightfully simple pastime we've stumbled into!

But here's the thing: Humans don't do simple. We just don't. Which, admittedly, has served us quite well when it comes to ventures such as space exploration, the internet, and Mexican pizza. But it doesn't do us a ton of favors when it comes to playing a friendly game involving a plastic ball.

We are a species that turned hobbyhorsing, air guitaring, and cheese rolling into competitive sports. So of course we weren't going to stand by and let pickleball remain uncomplicated.

Much like the progression seen with pickleball fashion (see chapter 4), gear has followed a trajectory, from humble to unhinged, in line with the unwritten rules of human obsession.

But unlike the many, and sometimes gradual, stages of pickleball fashion, players commonly go from "I got this cheap paddle off Amazon" to "This paddle has a honeycomb polymer core" in a disarmingly short amount of time. And that time usually starts about 4.7 seconds after a "super chill" player's fifth loss. The first four could be chalked up to newbie status, but number five? Now this is getting embarrassing. It's time to get serious about this thing.

Acquiring actual skill will take time, patience, and humility. But gear? Gear ships in two days.

And so begins the gear spiral. A treacherous path paved with core technology, compression sleeves, grip tape, and wildly overestimated potential. No one has ever been known to return from the spiral unscathed or free of credit card debt. But we push on,

PICKLEBALL GEAR

What You Think You Need: paddle, shoes, water.

What You End Up With: paddle (plus backup paddle, plus emotional support paddle), pickleball shoes, backup pickleball shoes, wristbands, towel, paddle bag, hat, visor, wicking shirt, sunglasses, grip tape, knee brace, hydration mix, energy chews, and a bumper sticker that reads, "Oops, I Dinked It Again."

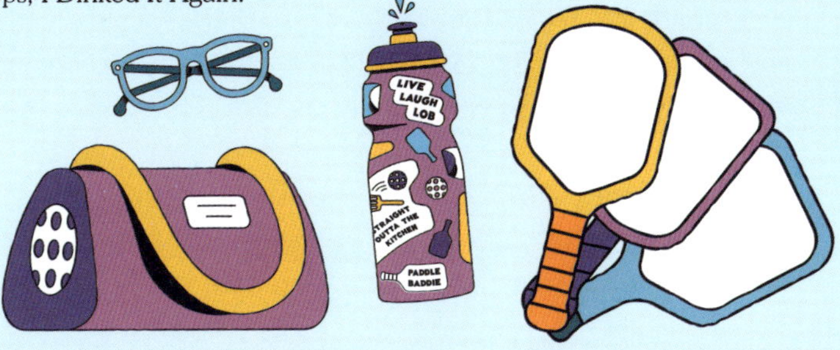

because the truth is, accumulating gear feels like progress. Like control. Like maybe the next time you step on the court, you'll be ready.

Will all this gear help you win? Maybe.

Will it give you something tangible to blame when you lose? Absolutely.

Let's gear up, shall we?

The Paddle Arms Race

No one starts with the right paddle. They start with the $39.99 beginner set that comes with two paddles, four balls, and a mesh bag that disintegrates on contact with sunlight. It's fine—until you lose to someone with a paddle that sounds more expensive.

TOP 5 PADDLE JUSTIFICATIONS

1. **"This paddle just isn't broken in yet." (It's brand-new and somehow already the problem.)**

2. **"It's more of a *power* paddle, and I needed *touch* today." (Bold of you to assume either skill was even near your performance.)**

3. **"The sweet spot is smaller on this one." (It's hard to hit the sweet spot when the ball doesn't even touch the paddle . . .)**

4. **"I forgot I switched paddles yesterday." (You are probably going to need to switch skill levels too . . .)**

5. **"This one doesn't give me enough spin." (Physics has given up on trying to help you.)**

That's when you dive headfirst into Paddle Research Hell. You become an amateur physicist overnight. You take note that you need a paddle that maximizes energy return and spin potential, has anti-vibration dampening, a honeycomb polymer core, a raw carbon face, torque acceleration and optimized twist weight, an aero-optimized edge guard, high grit surface, the right amount of dwell and deflection, a thick core, or maybe a thin core, and thermo-formed edge technology, with the best sweet spot.

You emerge seventy-two hours later, bleary-eyed and $229 poorer, clutching a high-end paddle named something like the SpinCycle 3000 XT HyperForce. It is confusingly endorsed by a 1990s sitcom actor who has never played pickleball but goes all in for the promo shots.

And . . . you still lose. Spectacularly. But now you lose with science on your side. You lose with technology. You lose with the unshakable belief that, someday, you and your overpriced paddle will rise together . . . just as the sitcom star promised.

Footwear: The Sole of the Game

Your shoes are the unsung heroes of your pickleball game. While your paddle gets all the glory and your knee brace (see page 66) gets all the sympathy, your footwear is the only thing standing between you and an appearance in a YouTube compilation titled "Pickleball Face Splats: Volume 6." In the beginning, you think any old sneakers will do. Running shoes, gym shoes, that worn down pair you throw on when you get the mail in the rain . . . they are all fine, right?

Wrong. You'll start out your pickleball adventure by wearing your old running shoes. They're comfy. They've got mileage. They're . . . a terrible idea. Because running shoes are designed for forward motion, and pickleball is a sport of lateral movement, quick stops, and sudden bursts of midlife regret. And nothing will humble you faster than trying to chase down a dink while your "athletic footwear" spontaneously gives up on this particular athletic endeavor.

You need court shoes, specifically built for side-to-side mayhem and stylish enough that someone might mistakenly think you know what you're doing. You need a shoe engineered for just enough bounce to trick your joints into thinking they're still twenty-five years old. Otherwise, you're one bad pivot away from becoming a cautionary tale. Today's pickleball shoes come with features you never even knew you needed: lateral support, pivot-enhancing treads, moisture-wicking insoles, ego-boosting color schemes. Some even claim to "maximize agility," which is adorable because, let's be honest, your maximum agility peaked somewhere around high school gym class, and even then, it was not exactly top of the class.

Look for court shoes: tennis, volleyball, or actual pickleball-specific shoes if you're feeling particularly professional.

Key features to consider:

- ***Lateral support*** **(so your ankles don't collapse like your self-esteem when lunging for a cross-court dink)**
- ***Grippy soles*** **(because uncontrolled sliding is less "athlete" and more "baby deer on frozen pond")**
- ***Stability and cushioning*** **(because your knees have a breaking point, and spoiler: you're closer to it than you think)**

Try them on. Move side to side as if you're dodging someone selling a multilevel marketing scheme. If your toes jam forward or your heels feel like you're bouncing on bad decisions, abandon ship. Also, don't pick a shoe that is a size up from your regular shoe size. That's how ankles disintegrate.

A BRIEF HISTORY OF SWEATBANDS

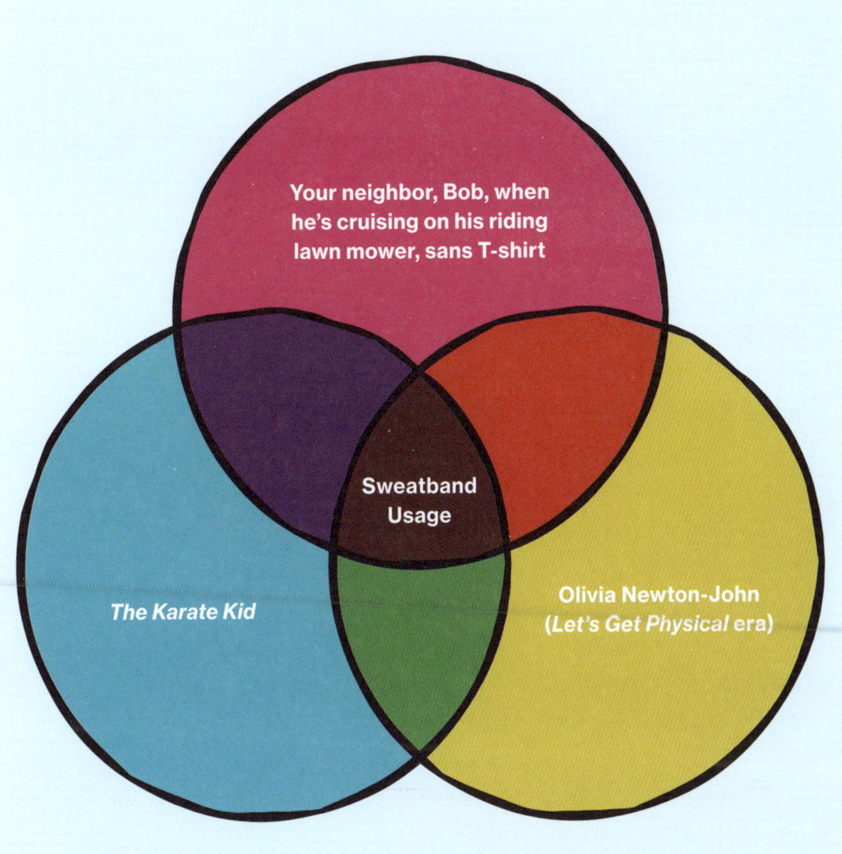

Once you have court shoes, you will immediately feel morally superior to anyone still sliding around in worn-out cross-trainers. You will side-eye. You will judge. You will believe (deep down) that your shoes will guide you to championship-level greatness. (They won't. But it's nice to dream.)

Your paddle might get all the attention, but it's your shoes that keep you upright, mobile, and marginally dignified. Choose wisely, or prepare to ice your regrets, one swollen ankle at a time.

Knee Braces, Elbow Sleeves, and Full Tactical Gear for a Friendly Tuesday Night Rec Game

At a certain point, pickleball stops feeling like a fun afternoon activity and starts feeling like a poorly planned gladiator match. One minute, you're laughing and dinking; the next, someone fires a ball directly into your spleen and trots away while you quietly contemplate your own mortality.

Not long after, your body stages its first quiet rebellion. A tiny twist in your lower back as you stretch for a ball just beyond your reach. A suspicious jolt in your ankle that wasn't there yesterday.

Then comes the true reckoning: waking up the morning after a recreational league match feeling as though you survived a WWE event—specifically the part where someone gets a folding chair broken across their back for dramatic effect.

That's when your body, wise beyond your bravado, develops a preemptive fear of serious injuries. Your ankles start sending polite warning signals. Your knees draft resignation letters. Your elbows quietly google "What is tendinitis?" You haven't even sustained a serious injury yet, but somehow, your soul already knows it's coming.

Enter: *the Brace Phase.*

BODY PARTS COMMONLY BRACED DURING PICKLEBALL

Knee braces. Ankle braces. Elbow sleeves. Wrist supports. Thumb stabilizers. You name a joint, there is a pickleballer bracing it. Not because they necessarily need to, but because doing so says, "I am an experienced warrior in this suburban battlefield."

OTHER GEAR THAT PROMISES PICKLEBALL GLORY

1. **High-friction grip tape:** Because apparently sweaty palms are why you're losing.
2. **Paddle lead tape:** For when adding weight sounds easier than fixing your swing.
3. **Cooling towels:** Heatstroke has never looked so fashionable.
4. **Electrolyte gummies:** You could probably also just eat three bags of cotton candy and hope your sugar high makes you a court menace.
5. **Paddle edge guards:** You have a $250 paddle and a $7.50 skill level . . . might as well throw some guards on there to protect your investment from yourself.
6. **Ball picker upper tubes:** Fetch balls faster, so you can get back to the losing quicker.
7. **Mini fans:** Clip-on breezes for those who want to channel their inner "Beyoncé in a music video" while playing.
8. **Court-specific sunglasses:** Because all your misses were totally the sun's fault.
9. **Weighted training paddles:** Perfect for your Pickleball Training Montage.
10. **Grip powder:** For the player who needs to feel like LeBron before every serve (add in a dramatic powder throw to really intimidate the other team).
11. **Court bags the size of a small SUV:** Carry your dreams . . . and quite a few postgame snacks.

The most common support seen among the warriors is the knee brace. Is it medical? Maybe. Is it psychological? Definitely.

Even if you don't need one yet, eventually you most definitely will. Or at least you'll convince yourself you do the moment you feel (and hear) your knee give its first warning sign of impending doom. Your mind says you are a warrior, but your knees know you are one lunge away from being the poster player for "F Around and Find Out." (To be honest, all your joints are in a race for which will be first to "find out.") So you throw on a brace and a prayer. It's in God's hands now.

Wearing a knee brace tells the court:

- **"I've been through some things, and I survived."**
- **"I'm most likely going to groan a lot every time I lunge for a ball."**
- **"If I miss said ball, I'm most likely going to adjust my knee brace, as an excuse."**
- **"Every match is a thrilling game of 'Will My ACL Hold?'"**
- **"I visit Costco every week just to purchase an industrial-sized container of ibuprofen."**

And some players wear so much neoprene (a stretchy, supportive, synthetic rubber material) that it's hard to tell if they're playing pickleball or gearing up for a deep-sea expedition. Elbow sleeves, wrist supports, elbow straps, back support, calf sleeves: all designed to cradle your joints in sweaty, overconfident protection while making you look as if you are trying out for a knockoff superhero movie.

Neoprene has been around for a while, but companies now make "pickleball-specific" neoprene gear, because apparently the sport requires its own level of physical and emotional support. Need extra compression for your forearm after your twelfth missed serve? Done. Calf tight from lunging at a ball you had no business chasing?

HOW *NOT* TO GEAR

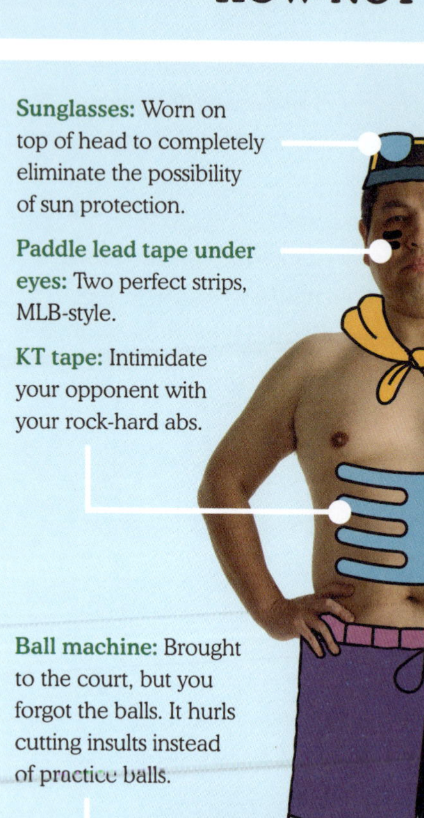

Sunglasses: Worn on top of head to completely eliminate the possibility of sun protection.

Paddle lead tape under eyes: Two perfect strips, MLB-style.

KT tape: Intimidate your opponent with your rock-hard abs.

Ball machine: Brought to the court, but you forgot the balls. It hurls cutting insults instead of practice balls.

Electrolyte powder pouch: Emptied directly into your mouth without water. You cough a lot. All in the name of proper hydration.

Grip tape headband: When you want to make a fashion statement, and lose quite a bit of hair.

Cooling towel: Worn as a cape. You are a superhero, so you must dress the part.

iPhone recording for AI evaluation of game: Phone facing the wrong way. Only records disturbing audio of grunts, wheezes, and curse words.

Crocs: Lime green. In sport mode. What could go wrong?

Leg warmers: Who needs compression socks when you have this much style?

There's a sleeve for that, too. Your thumb feeling a little wobbly in the wind while playing? Get it under control with wrist and thumb support. Whether you actually need these products or just want to look like you're sponsored by a medical supply company, neoprene will proudly cling to you through every questionable on-court decision.

And let's not forget compression socks. Ostensibly for circulation and performance, they mostly serve to declare, "I've read several blogs." There's also kinesiology tape—the duct tape of athletic optimism, it lets everyone know you've watched one too many TikToks about pickleball recovery.

Finally, you're barely sweating, but you've got three sweatbands on. One on each wrist. One across your forehead. You have more than one set. They make you look . . . committed. Do they help? Unclear. Do they make you feel like the star of a feel-good sports drama about a scrappy underdog who steals hearts and championships? Absolutely.

Most of us wear all this gear because it helps us pretend we're survivors of many a pickleball skirmish. And deep down, we know: It won't take anything dramatic to move us from traction (on the court) to traction (in a hospital bed). So we brace for impact.

The Most Underrated Gear on the Court: Snacks

Sure, paddles, shoes, and compression sleeves protect your body on the court, but let us not forget the gear that will cement your status off the court as well. And that is the most important gear of all: the postgame snack spread. Because you might not have the best serve or the quickest feet, but you know what you can have? An ice chest that opens like a treasure chest of popularity and refrigerated glory. Cue the inspirational music!

ULTIMATE SNACK MVP TOOLKIT

- **Rolling cooler:** Maybe with some sparkly lights around the wheels?
- **Paper plates and napkins:** We are civilized and are not using our paddles as plates.
- **Tongs and toothpicks:** Keep gross hands away from victory snacks.
- **Hand sanitizer:** Perhaps enough to spread over everyone's entire postgame body.
- **Foldable table:** Let's elevate this situation.
- **Trash bag or bin:** Keep it clean.
- **Bluetooth speaker and/or old-school boom box:** To bring the vibes.

Snack-O-Meter

Individual bags of chips and/or pretzels Basic, but gets the job done.

Cookies and/or mini cupcakes Store-bought and a sure thing.

Veggie and hummus cups Individual cups of hummus with veggies on top. To balance out the cupcakes.

Orange slices Bring back memories of childhood rec games with this nostalgic fan favorite.

Pinwheel sandwiches Like Mom used to make for the neighborhood Fourth of July party.

ASSEMBLING A LEGENDARY POSTGAME LINEUP

If you want to be a true pickleball champion, you need to be a person who is there to play, yes, but also a person who is ready to snack, socialize, and secure lifelong friendships through the shared experience of excessive caloric intake.

But one cannot simply roll up with a couple of protein bars and expect to be greeted with instant adoration. There are important details to take into consideration before striving for snack superiority. Let us discuss them now.

How to Serve the Best Snack Spread

- ***Plan Ahead*** Don't show up with a rogue sleeve of saltines and your kids' leftover fruit snacks and call it a spread. Snack greatness requires intention, and possibly a dedicated album on your phone with inspo photos.
- ***Bring Variety*** Sweet to recover. Salt to replenish. Cheese because . . . well, everyone needs cheese. Crunch to drown out the sound of your worn joints popping.
- ***Consider Portability*** No one wants to eat mac 'n' cheese out of a bowl that is balancing on a dusty paddle. Think finger foods and grab-and-go greatness.
- ***Remember, Everyone Is Gross*** Pickleball is sweaty. Bodies are sweaty after playing pickleball. Hands are part of those bodies. And we don't need gross sweaty hands spreading gross sweatiness throughout the delicious snack spread. Stick to snacks that can isolate everyone's gross sweatiness to their own treats. Worst-case scenario, at least bring tongs or toothpicks to cut down on hands coming into contact with shared food. Also, avoid snacks that could possibly result in a double dip situation, because that can be a pain to police and hard to enforce if you are snacking with overzealous dippers.

- ***Label If Needed*** **Throw allergy warnings on anything that may turn your postgame fun into an unfortunate ambulance ride.**
- ***Leave No Crumb Behind*** **Pack up, wipe down, and leave the court better than you found it. Don't be the buzzkill who trashes the court for the next players/snackers.**

All the Apps

Once a player hits peak pickleball obsession, the apps start creeping in. Why just play, accessorize, and socialize when you can also analyze, overthink, and hyperfixate on the hobby you swore was "just for fun"?

Pickleball apps are everywhere, promising players very little except the ability to spend as much time as humanly possible obsessing over pickle play. There are apps to track stats, analyze swings, find local courts, connect with other players, schedule matches, and even live stream your games—an exciting development for the poor coworkers already being held hostage by your watercooler match recaps.

Many apps now allow players to upload footage of their games so AI can critique their every move like a disapproving Olympic coach. Because nothing says "great use of technology" than watching a slow-motion replay confirmation of our own athletic mediocrity.

Whatever tiny sliver of simplicity pickleball still has left, don't worry—there's definitely an app ready to swoop in and overcomplicate it for you.

MOST COMMON DATA FROM PICKLEBALL APPS

Serve accuracy	**12%** (but delivered with unwavering ***swagger***)
Average heart rate	**Elevated**, mostly from arguing line calls 
Percentage of match spent thinking about postgame snacks	**48%**
Steps per match 	**2,400**, most of them pacing in frustration and/or chasing after the ball you missed
Time spent blaming equipment	**42%** (and ***rising***)
Paddle speed	***Just fast enough to miss the ball***
Number of unforced errors	Emotionally ***devastating***, statistically ***impressive*** 
Spin calculations	Less ball rotation, more you spinning yourself like a top after a dramatic swing
Energy output 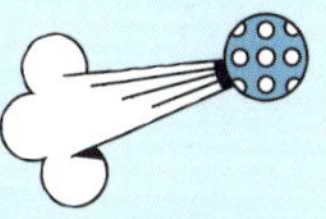	**43%** dramatic sighing, **27%** exasperation, **11%** hopes, **13%** instant regret, **6%** actual gameplay
Recovery time	Three to five business days

6

THE PICKLE PEOPLE

A Field Guide to the Personalities of Pickle

A new pickleball player might assume that once they master the rules, jargon, fashion, and gear, they will have the sport pretty much figured out. But it is not long before every newbie comes to understand the true challenge of the game: the people who play it. The court is an ecosystem unto itself, teeming with life-forms as varied as those found on a wilderness safari. From apex predators who stalk to the kitchen line to wide-eyed wanderers chasing balls like newborn cubs after butterflies, the pickleball court is nature's weirdest walkabout. Welcome to the Pickle Jungle.

The longer an observer spends in the wilds of the pickleball court, the more distinct characters emerge from the chaos. The boisterous, the quiet, the social, the outlandishly intense. They congregate around courts like herds to watering holes, armed with protective eyewear, hydration backpacks, and an unshakable belief that they are the only normal ones out here.

This chapter serves as your essential field guide—a critical survival tool for navigating the wild terrain of pickleball. I'll identify the dominant species, explore their habitats and behaviors, and offer handy tips for coexisting with these colorful oddballs. Whether you're a seasoned court naturalist or a first-time explorer, one thing is certain: No trek through the land of pickleball is without an assortment of characters. Proceed with caution, the ability to dodge both a ball or an awkward conversation, and maybe some electrolyte gummies to throw at the wildlife. Let's meet the Pickle People.

Sergeant Serious

Professor Paddle

The Social Butterfly

The "Rusty" Ringer

Captain Constructive Criticism

The Cub

The Ball Hog

The Silent Storm

SERGEANT SERIOUS

Habitat Forever glued to the kitchen line. Ready to attack, ready to defend, ready to win.

Mating call "That's out!" (wailed well in advance of said ball being out).

Distinguishing features Fingerless gloves, knee/shoulder/ankle/thumb braces engaged and ready for battle, sunglasses with no lenses (none of the fogging potential, all the eye protection), four different paddles, an endless collection of pickleball-themed performance shirts.

Behavioral notes Approaches casual rec play with the intensity of a bomb defusal expert and views smiling during gameplay as a sign of weakness; just an overall blast to be around.

Handling instructions In order to survive an encounter with this personality, you must play with reckless joy and zero strategy. Celebrate wildly after every completely lucky shot. Sergeant Serious can handle tough opponents, but watching you "just vibe" on the court will short-circuit his game plan.

PROFESSOR PADDLE

Habitat Standing near the fence, casually cornering unsuspecting victims into TED talks about paddle composition.

Mating call "Honestly, your paddle is costing you at least three points a game."

Distinguishing features Owns seventeen paddles, rotates them like wine pairings. Wears a moisture-wicking shirt featuring the logo of a paddle company no one's heard of—one of about twenty she scored at the Pickle Paddle Power Convention.

Behavioral notes Judges your paddle with the quiet disdain of a sommelier inspecting boxed wine. Allows you to hold her paddles as though you are being offered a chance to kiss the Stanley Cup.

Handling instructions Nod with reverence. Pretend you are "in the research phase of upgrading" even if you are holding firm with your $39 paddle from Walmart. It's the only way to escape without a forty-five-minute lecture.

THE SOCIAL BUTTERFLY

Habitat Somehow always finds the only patch of shade on the court or brings their own umbrella to create a welcoming spot for others to congregate. Usually comes bearing snacks, folding chairs, and high fives.

Mating call "We should totally get brunch after this!" (blurted out during opponent's serve).

Distinguishing features Permanent coffee cup in hand, pickleball bag with an easily accessible pocket for their phone. They need to grab said phone frequently to coordinate calendar availability with new friends. Knows everyone's birthdays, dogs' names, and recent medical history.

Behavioral notes Spends about 20% of their time playing pickleball and 80% of their time mingling, networking, and adding people to group text strings.

Handling instructions Lean into it. They're the glue that holds the community together. If you need to get a game started, try promising, "Let's knock this game out, and then we can huddle up on the best happy hour in the area."

THE "RUSTY" RINGER

Habitat Sideline, stretching theatrically while casually announcing they "haven't played in months."

Mating call "Wait, how do you call the score again?"

Distinguishing features Gives off "just here for fun" vibes and a serve that can't help but give them away.

Behavioral notes Self-deprecating and silly—until they rip five unreturnable shots into your torso.

Handling instructions Side-eye the false modesty. The ringer will not be even a little bit rusty, so come out of the gate ready to rumble.

CAPTAIN CONSTRUCTIVE CRITICISM

Habitat Hovering, arms crossed, at the sideline of any court, at any time, always uninvited.

Mating call "Mind if I give you some feedback?" (does not wait for the answer before giving feedback).

Distinguishing features Wears a backward hat, mirrored sunglasses, and the swagger of a 1970s gym teacher.

Behavioral notes Turns every casual game into an opportunity to spread the Power of Proper Pickle™. Fueled by 400+ hours of YouTube drills and that one time they came from nine points down to pull off an upset win.

Handling instructions Nod enthusiastically and pretend to take mental notes. Do not ask follow-up questions. If necessary, fake a highly contagious disease: "I'm planning to work on my backhand as soon as I get this pink eye cleared up."

THE CUB

Habitat Wandering aimlessly between courts with a borrowed paddle and shoes that scream inevitable ankle injury.

Mating call "Wait, why do we switch sides after each serve?"

Distinguishing features Yoga pants, a T-shirt their mom brought back from a cruise to Barbados, and "athletic" shoes that have never been near anything athletic in their long, lazy life.

Behavioral notes Endearingly enthusiastic but dangerously unpredictable. Sometimes trips over the kitchen line, sometimes channels their inner Serena Williams—it's anyone's guess what version is showing up for each serve. And you never know what "newbie" went to college on a tennis scholarship and is four points away from figuring out how to translate their dormant skills.

Handling instructions Patience. Lots of it. Laugh off the fumbles and celebrate the completely unintentional successes. We were all Cubs once, and this one could be schooling you by next week with their untapped pickle precision.

THE BALL HOG

Habitat Center court, always. Ready, waiting, overcompensating.
Mating call "I GOT IT! IT'S MINE!"
Distinguishing features Rocks a knee brace and the stance of a goalie during penalty kicks in the World Cup final. Relentlessly swats at balls as if they're in a *Karate Kid*–type training montage.
Behavioral notes Believes the entire game will fall apart at the seams if they do not come into contact with 99.3% of balls hit to their team. Convinced they're "carrying the squad," though the heaviest thing on court is their ego.
Handling instructions Step aside and let them chase balls like an over-caffeinated Labrador. Maintain a five-foot safety radius at all times, because you never know when one of their overextended attempts at a hit will result in a paddle to your temple.

THE SILENT STORM

Habitat Drifts silently from sideline to sideline, never out of position, never saying a word.

Mating call None. Just a slight nod, a quick adjustment of their thumb guard, and then . . . annihilation.

Distinguishing features Rolls up to the court with only a top-of-the-line paddle and zero visible emotion. Dresses in all black; flair is not for finishers.

Behavioral notes Delivers cross-court shots with the calm of someone folding laundry and the precision of a trained sniper. A combo that feels both efficient and terrifying in equal measure.

Handling instructions Treat them like a sleeping dragon—stay respectful, stay quiet, and if you screw up, mourn the point like a soldier lost to the cause.

THE HONORABLE MENTIONS

The Excusinator	Blames every error on the paddle, the sun, the wind. The kind of player who instantly examines the court for abnormalities if they miss a ball.
The Injury Prone	Can't make it through a game without "aggravating an old injury." Also can't make it through the game without going into extreme detail about the injury and various medical treatments.
The Pickleball Fashionista	The sun reflecting off their bedazzled shorts provides their only legitimate defensive strategy.
The Rage Quitter	One minute they're fist-pumping like a champion, the next they're storming off the court as if someone insulted their ancestors—when really, they just couldn't handle going down 6–1. Their tantrums are the stuff of legends, spoken in hushed tones and wide eyes.
The Chronic Apologizer	Constantly apologizing for everything they, or anyone else, does incorrectly on the court.
The Court DJ	Brings a Bluetooth speaker and insists on turning the court into the world's least sexy rave.
The Spiritual Server	Takes thirty seconds before each serve to breathe deeply and align their chakras, then hits it straight into the net.
The Over-Applauder	Always ready with an enthusiastic round of applause and a completely unwarranted burst of positivity. Energy is a combination of reckless enthusiasm and a soccer coach for a team of five-year-olds.
The Snack Bar	Rolls up to the court (literally) with an ice chest full of beverages and a backpack full of calories. Ready to fuel. Ready to share. Ready to party.

At the end of the day, one of the most endearing qualities of pickleball is that it is accessible to such a broad assortment of people. This inclusion produces a wild and wonderful ecosystem overflowing with characters rarely found congregating together in nature. From the serious to the silly, and everyone in between, all the Pickle People play a role in keeping the courts colorful, chaotic, and deeply entertaining.

Yes, some will shout. Some will sparkle. Some will be emotionally invested in a way that feels more than a little unhealthy. But without them, pickleball would be . . . normal. Like televised golf normal. And we are not here for normal. We are here to pickle. So embrace the madness. High-five the Cub. Indulge Captain Constructive Criticism. Add your number to the Social Butterfly's group text. And above all, play your part, even if that part changes over time. Because there is room for everyone and every quirk out here in the Pickle Jungle. Even the over-celebrators, overdressers, and overexplainers. Especially them (especially if they are sharing snacks).

Pickleball Etiquette: How to Avoid Being *That* Person

Despite its growing popularity and rating systems (see page 138), pickleball still thrives on community. At its roots, it is a fun backyard game between friends. It's the kind of sport where strangers become pickup partners, matches can lead to friendships, and Tuesday night drop-ins turn into the highlight of someone's week. But sometimes players forget that they are essentially playing big ping-pong with a plastic ball, and they start to treat recreational play like a Navy SEALs training session. They coach their partners mid-rally, they argue line calls with the passion of Meryl Streep going for

PICKLEBALL *DOS* AND *DON'TS*

✓ ***DO*** **call the score clearly before each serve.**
✗ ***DON'T*** **yell it like an announcer at a monster truck rally.**

✓ ***DO*** **encourage your partner.**
✗ ***DON'T*** **coach them as though you're in a training montage they did not sign up for.**

✓ ***DO*** **call your own faults honestly.**
✗ ***DON'T*** **act as if your foot didn't land in the kitchen when everyone on the court saw it happen.**

✓ ***DO*** **celebrate your wins with class.**
✗ ***DON'T*** **launch into a pre-rehearsed dance that involves finger guns. (Worth noting: Finger guns are never okay, in pickleball or in life.)**

✓ ***DO*** **keep the game moving.**
✗ ***DON'T*** **take a water break, check your email, or get caught up on court gossip between points.**

✓ ***DO*** **keep your vibe positive.**
✗ ***DON'T*** **sigh, mutter, or give your partner the same look you give your puppy when he pees on the carpet.**

✓ ***DO*** **include new players.**
✗ ***DON'T*** **believe that pickleball is serious enough to be exclusive.**

✓ ***DO*** **bring snacks to share.**
✗ ***DON'T*** **bring something weird and mysterious in a Tupperware that smells like future food poisoning.**

✓ ***DO*** **dress for comfort and movement.**
✗ ***DON'T*** **treat the court like Coachella for middle-aged rec athletes.**

- ✓ *DO* be aware of your surroundings.
- ✗ *DON'T* accidentally clothesline your partner while swinging for a ball with what could only be described as half interpretive dance, half helicopter blade of doom.

- ✓ *DO* laugh off mistakes and have fun.
- ✗ *DON'T* blame the paddle, the sun, or your "old pitching elbow" for your mistakes. (We all know the only thing you've pitched lately is a light beer to your buddy at the neighborhood BBQ.)

- ✓ *DO* stay aware of the game on neighboring courts.
- ✗ *DON'T* chase your ball through someone else's rally as if you're racing to save the lead character in the final scene of a summer blockbuster.

- ✓ *DO* admit when you got lucky on a ridiculous shot.
- ✗ *DON'T* pretend it was all skill when your eyes were closed and everyone saw the ball bounce off your forehead.

- ✓ *DO* show up with a good attitude and a willingness to play with anyone.
- ✗ *DON'T* scan the court as though you are building an Olympic squad. Because spoiler alert: You are not.

- ✓ *DO* offer a friendly paddle tap or "good game" at the end.
- ✗ *DON'T* storm off as though a grand jury is being convened to investigate the injustices you've just experienced on the court.

her thirty-fifth Oscar nomination, they act like every missed ball is a dagger to their fragile heart. They are . . . a lot. And they are . . . most likely not going to be invited to hang out again.

Etiquette in pickleball is everything. It's what makes the sport feel welcoming, inclusive, and, above all else, fun. So it's time for a crash course in not being *that* person—the one who inspires a mass exodus every time they show up to the court. Because in pickleball, skill gets you points, but etiquette gets you partners and, more important, included in the group chat. Let's make sure you're not the player everyone ghosts by game two.

How *That* Person Celebrates

We've all seen it, we've all heard it, we've all cringed at it: the over-the-top victory celebration. It's the hallmark of many sports, from choreographed touchdown dances to shirts being ripped off post soccer goal. It's acceptable in stadiums, less so on your neighborhood pickleball court.

One of the fastest ways to ensure your membership in the *That* Person Club is to partake in a deliriously obnoxious celebration during a pickleball game. And if you do it after *every* point? Congrats, you're now a VIP member of the cringe club.

- ***Paddle Tap*** **A simple "good job" recognition. Flair add-ons (high five, paddle twirl, tap and salute) available with little offense taken by opponent.**
- ***Jump and Chest Bump*** **Seems like a good idea until middle-aged "athletes" realize they don't quite have the same vertical clearance they once had.**
- ***Slow-Mo Strut*** **Move in exaggerated slow motion for maximum effect/annoyance.**

- ***"Let's GOOOOOOO!"*** The go-to for ferocious competitors these days. Many have seen professional athletes scream out this phrase in exuberance and victory, and now they believe recreational sports are in need of the battle cry.
- ***Cartwheel Attempt*** Less a celebration than a predictor of a future rotator cuff surgery.
- ***Finger Guns + Wink Combo*** Just, no.
- ***Victory Lap*** Sprint around the court while your partner chases you like a camera man looking to get the hero shot.
- ***"Choreographed" Dance Routine*** Usually just ends up being two people gyrating to wildly different beats.
- ***Dirty Dancing*** Sure, this is obnoxious, but if they can actually stick the lift? Legends.

At its core, pickleball etiquette is simple: Don't be the reason someone needs to fake food poisoning and disappear mid-game. Play fair, be fun, and try to leave any and all fanatical tendencies at home. If you can pull that off, you'll never lack for partners, and most most important, for postgame snacks.

Next up, let's dive into how to pick a perfect partner (you're on your own for snack selection).

7

THE QUEST FOR THE PERFECT PICKLEBALL PARTNER

Courtship, Chemistry, and the Occasional Mid-Game Meltdown

Finding the perfect pickleball partner is a lot like dating, except with arguably more emotional breakdowns. You start off optimistic—paddle in hand, a heart full of hope—certain that your ideal match is out there waiting for their paddlemate to dink into their lives, too.

Just like dating apps, the search for the perfect partner can involve a lot of swipes and a lot of duds. And that's just during your first rally. You'll meet those who talk a big game and ghost you after meeting at open play, the emotionally stunted who rage through every point, and the well-meaning Cub who is still rattled each time they have to call the score. But somewhere in the mess of possible mates, maybe, just maybe, you'll find a partner who not only understands the game but also understands *you.*

At first you think, "Anyone who plays pickleball will make a great partner!" That, my friend, is more than a rookie mistake—it is the equivalent to marrying the first person you match with on a dating app, simply because they list *ALF* as their favorite TV show of all time. (Which, to be fair, is not the worst strategy for choosing a life partner—but let's stay focused.)

It only takes one disastrous match with a Ball Hog who screams "MINE!" at every ball (before the ball has even been served), or a Captain Constructive Criticism attempting to micromanage your backhand mid-point, before you realize: Choosing a partner isn't casual, it's an art. A trust fall of sorts, with a face-plant into the kitchen as your reward if you choose incorrectly.

Unfortunately, there's no app-like algorithm for finding perfect chemistry on the court. Compatibility is about attitude, communication, and a shared willingness to laugh after an unfortunate display of athletic mediocrity. It's about knowing they'll take the shot, not your self-esteem.

The truth is, a perfect pickleball partnership is rarer than a crowded court without a single splash of neon in sight. It doesn't happen often, but when it does, it's a thing of beauty: coordinated movements, silent communication, and a genuine, playful "Almost!" after you whiff an easy shot. You cover their middle, they cover your mistakes, and nobody passive-aggressively mutters, "Interesting choice," after your errant ball blasts into the net.

This chapter explores the good, the bad, and the downright awkward of pickleball partnerships, from the flirty singles mixer energy of open play to the on-court breakups that everyone pretends not to be staring at. From the boisterous to the bizarre, I've cataloged the common archetypes, red flags, and survival tips that will help you find the perfect partner, or barring that, at least the player who has the best postgame snacks in their paddle bag.

Surprisingly Great
PICKLEBALL PARTNER COMBOS

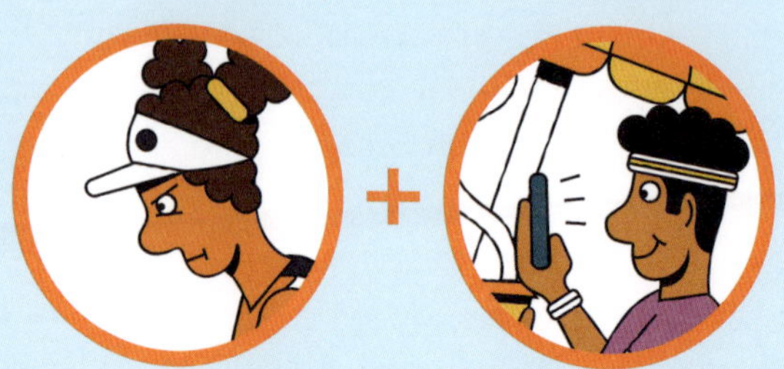

The Silent Storm and The Social Butterfly

Why it works: One brings laser focus, the other brings lunch plans.
Dynamic: They are both cool, but one in an icy sort of way and the other in a coordinating team shirts sort of way.
Bonus: The Social Butterfly disarms opponents with banter while the Silent Storm disarms them with a ruthless backhand.

Captain Constructive Criticism and The Social Butterfly

Why it works: The Social Butterfly softens the Captain's sharp edges.
Dynamic: Both have strong opinions—one about pickleball, the other about group selfies.
Bonus: It's hard for the Captain to come up with much to criticize about the postgame snacks provided by the Butterfly.

Sergeant Serious and The Cub

Why it works: Discipline meets raw enthusiasm.
Dynamic: The Sergeant brings structure, the Cub brings mayhem. They balance each other.
Bonus: If the Cub is an eager one, they could level up quickly under the rigid wing of Sergeant Serious.

Professor Paddle and The "Rusty" Ringer

Why it works: One has all the gear, the other has all the game.
Dynamic: Data nerd meets street (or court) smarts.
Bonus: They'll win, and only one of them will pretend this is surprising.

Combos to Avoid

BALL HOG + SERGEANT SERIOUS = full-blown turf war.

SOCIAL BUTTERFLY + SOCIAL BUTTERFLY = their score will be a disaster, but their postgame mimosa flight will be on point.

CAPTAIN CONSTRUCTIVE CRITICISM + PROFESSOR PADDLE = nobody has fun, and the games take three business days to complete because the two of them can't shut up long enough to actually play.

The Pros and Cons of the Pickle People

Not all partners are created equal. Some bring out the best in you and others make you dream of pushing them into the kitchen mid-rally. As you are on the lookout for your forever match, consult this handy pros-and-cons breakdown of some Pickle People you may date along the way.

Sergeant Serious (see page 80) **Partner with them if you work well under pressure and think rec sports should be less rec and more ROTC.**

Pros: Your reflexes will get honed not only from the in-game play, but also from the insults being hurled your way.
Cons: Please see "Pros."

Professor Paddle (see page 81) **There are so many options when it comes to paddles, how could you ever have time to research them all? Enter . . . your very own walking Google search!**

Pros: Access to a curated paddle collection and so much more information about surface textures than you could ever accumulate in your lifetime.
Cons: Every game error could result in a paddle-blaming explanation longer than most podcasts.

The Social Butterfly (see page 82) **When you are first starting out in the pickle world, it never hurts to know the player who knows all the other players. Think of the Social Butterfly as your rebound partner of sorts. They'll help you get your footing**

in this new environment and boost your confidence until you find your forever partner.

> *Pros:* Who doesn't enjoy high fives, new friends, and getting invited to a brunch meet-up before the third game starts?
> *Cons:* Don't be surprised if they reply to a text mid-rally.

The "Rusty" Ringer ***(see page 83)*** **Sometimes it is worth the gamble to partner up with the player dramatically feigning to be "out of practice."**

> *Pros:* It usually doesn't take them long to slip right back "into practice," via a sniper of a serve.
> *Cons:* It may become very clear, very quickly, that their "rusty" is still miles ahead of your "absolute, we are talking the stars are perfectly aligned, best."

Captain Constructive Criticism ***(see page 84)*** **Maybe you are ready to fully commit to becoming a student of the sport. Maybe your self-esteem has been feeling a little too esteemed lately. Maybe you've always had a thing for gym teachers.**

> *Pros:* Private lessons are expensive; constructive criticism is free!
> *Cons:* May be sporting a clipboard. Unironically.

The Cub ***(see page 85)*** **Like partnering with, well, a cub. Enthusiastic, playful, and often mid-celebration before the point is over.**

> *Pros:* You just never know when a moment of accidental brilliance may occur.
> *Cons:* Boundless energy, limited awareness.

The Ball Hog (see page 86) **If you are someone who freezes when the ball comes your way, I have just the partner for you!**

Pros: You'll enjoy all the cardio of a regular pickleball game, without any of the pressure to actually hit a ball.
Cons: Most of the cardio comes from sprinting to avoid collisions and dodging wild paddle swings.

The Silent Storm (see page 87) **If you're looking for victory without the distracting flare of smiles and joy, this is your partner.**

Pros: You will win games.
Cons: You will never, ever high-five.

Match Point: Picking Your Pickleball Person

Like any great rom-com, you're going to need to endure a montage of terrible matches and unforced errors before finding "the one."

STEP ONE: THE FIRST DATE (AKA OPEN PLAY)

Open play is a casual drop-in session where players rotate through games with whoever's available. In most open play scenarios, no partner is necessary, just a paddle and a willingness to mingle. It is the speed dating of pickleball–equal parts hopeful and horrifying. You show up with optimism, ready to find your courtmate, or at least someone who will make this forced socialization marginally more entertaining than the Netflix binge you abandoned at home. You might leave the event googling "solo hobbies with no small talk" and dodging eye contact from the That One Guy who has been hovering in your general vicinity since you arrived.

It's where you meet:

Vibe Vinnie **Who shows up wearing, and insists on playing with, earbuds and a fanny pack. There is an 86% chance that his pregame brownie is fueling him with something a little stronger than just carbohydrates.**

Back-in-Tennis Brenda **Who reminds you every 34.2 seconds of her glory years spent owning the tennis court.**

Stat Steve **Who brings a notebook, tracks each game like a scientist conducting a career-defining study, and has more pickleball apps on his phone than photos of his immediate family.**

Mood Swing Martha **Who goes from jovial and fun to disarmingly invested in the outcome of one tough rally in the span of a millisecond. You're not quite sure if you are going to get a judgmental scowl or a reassuring smile if you miss a ball. Martha is not sure either.**

Going Through Something Gary **Who mistakenly believes people actually want to know the answer when they ask, "How's it going?" Coping with heartbreak, an existential crisis, or both, his misdirected angst results in a deep, troubling investment in every single point.**

Open play is where sparks might fly, or where chemistry may evaporate in a sad scene involving hubris and humiliation (with a side of good old-fashioned complete and utter personality mismatch). Just like dating, you might have to endure a lot of metaphorical frogs (complete with confusing hopping and manic swiping at things in the air) to find your match at open play. But keep your mind open, your backhand ready, and a faux injury chambered in case you need an exit strategy: "I hope I can make it through the games tonight! My tibia [or fibula or any other word you remember from high school biology class] has been acting up!"

STEP TWO: THE COMPATIBILITY TEST

So, you've found someone who might be worth a second pickleball date. Congrats! Now it's time to go a little deeper into compatibility. Because not all pickles ball equally. That's why the number one rule of finding the right partner is this: Find the right partner for *you.* This may sound obvious, but many people get caught up in how a player looks on paper and spend less time worrying about how the player feels . . . *in the heart.*

Maybe you are a Social Butterfly who needs someone more serious to counter your verve for selfies. Maybe you are a Sergeant Serious who needs someone who doesn't get offended by your very offensive-looking game face. Maybe you are a Captain Constructive Criticism who needs someone who doesn't cry easily.

Pickleball partnership is about a lot more than winning or losing. It's about the ability of each partner to win or lose with a similar intensity, sense of humor, and/or coordinated socks.

Questions When Picking a Potential Partner

- **Do they warm up, or just wander onto the court two minutes before the start of the game wearing flip-flops and drinking an iced latte?**
- **Do they say, "Nice try" or just "Why, though?"**
- **Do they respect the kitchen rules or seem utterly baffled every time they get called for a fault (while standing in the middle of said kitchen)?**
- **Do they announce the score or scream it as if they are calling the kids in for supper in the 1950s?**
- **Do they yell, "Yours!" about 0.2 seconds before they miss a ball?**
- **Do they compliment the other team on good shots or simply hang their head in disgust when faced with skill on the other side of the net?**
- **Do they seem as though they are here to have fun or to defend their family name via pickleball play?**
- **Do they mumble encouragements or criticism under their breath between points?**
- **Do they discuss a strategy or expect Jedi-like mind reading skills?**
- **Do they offer you good snacks after the game?**

PARTNERING WITH YOUR ACTUAL PARTNER

(Spouse / Significant Other)

What could be better than sharing a court with the person who also shares your heart? And how unbeatable will the two of you be out there? You'll have silent communication, seamless teamwork, and the envy of all who are unfortunate enough to face your unstoppable dynamic. What an experience this will be!

But. Also. This could go very, very wrong. There is a reason that "pickleball divorce" is rapidly becoming a leading cause of marriage turbulence throughout the land.

Turns out, compatibility in love doesn't guarantee compatibility in a doubles match. You may split bills, raise kids, and even share a Costco membership, but none of that prepares you for being down 8 to 3 when one of you has just served into the net. Nothing exposes cracks in a relationship quite like a recreational sport with an inflated sense of importance.

Playing pickleball with your spouse can be a beautiful way to grow your relationship or a horrible idea that marks a sweaty end to your love story. It's equal parts teamwork and tension, fun and fuming. Not every couple is built for shared court time, and that's okay. You can still love someone and never want to be near their awkward post-point running man dance ever again.

But if you are going to head out on the court together and also want to head home in the same car, remember these tips: Keep a sense of humor, be each other's biggest fan, and give each other grace if the heat of competition brings out a slightly different version of each of you. You are not just playing pickleball together—you're practicing patience, communication, and conflict resolution in matching dry-fit shorts.

And any couple who can sweat in neon together is for sure going the distance.

Relationship Issues, Now with Athleisure!

- ***Time Management Tension:*** "I see you can make time for pickleball, but not dinner with my mother."
- ***Passive-Aggressive Parade:*** "No worries, I'll just get every ball like I do everything else in this marriage."
- ***Shot-Calling = Life Commentary:*** "You try to control everything, in life and on the court!"
- ***Unexpected Rage Issues:*** "Why are you screaming and throwing your paddle? I guess it *is* possible for you to get more upset than when Trader Joe's discontinued your favorite frozen appetizers."
- ***Conflict Avoidance:*** "Never *mind.* I don't want to talk about why that point upset me."
- ***Selective Hearing Syndrome:*** "I said *yours* three times. Just like I've told you not to leave dishes in the sink three million times. Both ignored."
- ***Communication Breakdown:*** "Just use your words! I can't read your mind!"
- ***The Power Struggle:*** "Why are you hovering all the time? Stay in your lane, Brad."
- ***Scorekeeping:*** "I've made all the points and all the sacrifices in this relationship. Just saying."
- ***The Postgame Debrief Turned Therapy Session:*** "Let's talk about our serves and our lack of emotional connection lately."

Pickleball chemistry isn't about skill; it's about vibe. If you're the type who treats rec play like an Olympic qualifier, you'll want a partner who doesn't flinch at a little intensity. If you are mostly out here to sweat and socialize, make sure your partner also prioritizes a good time over a good serve.

There are countless ways to pickle: competitive, casual, chaotic, caffeinated. Just make sure your partner is not only on the same court as you, but also playing the same version of the game. Otherwise, you'll both be swinging in the wind, with not a sync in sight.

STEP THREE: COMMUNICATION STYLES

As in any relationship, communication is the main ingredient to a successful match. You don't necessarily need to have exactly the same communication style as your partner, but the two of you do need to be able to sync up on the court without the need for an interpreter and/or an intervention.

Here are some of the ways in which picklers ponder:

The Loud and Proud **Calls every ball, every play, every minor shift in wind direction.**

The Underbreath Whisperer **They have a lot of thoughts, but you can't actually hear any of them.**

The Moaner **Sighs, groans, and mutters through the game. Sometimes about the playing, sometimes about their sore back, always in a way that makes everyone in the general vicinity concerned.**

The Over-Encourager **Not so much communication as a wall of motivational posters come to life.**

The Huddle Upper **Wants a team meeting after every point. You're a little worried they may suggest an off-site team building retreat in the near future.**

The Scoreboard Announcer **States the score at every opportunity. Louder each time. Possibly unaware that this is rec play, not Monday Night Football.**

Wordless Wonder **No words, no drama. They say everything with a quick nod or slight smile. A little intimidating, but a lot effective.**

STEP FOUR: IT'S A MATCH! (MAYBE.)

In the end, finding the perfect pickleball partner is less about skills and strategy and more about shared energy, solid communication, and whether the two of you can lose a game without causing a full-court emotional meltdown. It's a wild mix of timing, temperament, and occasionally, good old-fashioned dumb luck—just like dating.

Sometimes it works. Sometimes it crashes into the net in spectacular fashion. But every match, win or lose, teaches you a little more about who you are as a player and what kind of partner brings out the best in you, both in your performance and in your enjoyment.

So choose wisely. Forgive quickly. And above all: Never, ever partner with someone who refers to themselves in the third person during warm-ups.

THE PERFECT PARTNER

Behold: The Perfect Partner. Built from the strongest parts of each pickle personality, this ideal teammate covers every shot, encourages every miss, and always, always brings snacks.

1. Sergeant Serious's military-caliber focus and strategy.
2. The "Rusty" Ringer's overly dramatic elbow brace lulls opponents into a false sense of security, right before that "injured" arm annihilates every ball that comes its way.
3. Tattoo = Irrationally committed to the cause.
4. A Ball Hog is always prepared.
5. The Spiritual Server (see page 88) must kiss this necklace and say a silent prayer before each serve. And quite frankly, our team could use all the help (spiritual or otherwise) we can get.
6. The Silent Storm's silent staredown.
7. The Social Butterfly boosts morale and captures every moment.
8. The Overly Braced: Are they injury prone or overly dramatic? Either way brings a little excitement to the team.
9. Professor Paddle brings her overpriced equipment that is engineered for glory.
10. Captain Constructive Criticism is here to help.
11. The Cub will most likely end up in urgent care with these shoes, but damn if they don't bring a ton of energy and zest to the game before needing medical attention.

6
1
2
10
FEEDBACK IS MY LOVE LANGUAGE.
5
3
DINK DADDY
4
7
8
11
9

8

THE STRATEGIES, OR WHERE CONFIDENCE OUTSHINES COMPETENCE

A Deep Dive into Pickleball's Most Confusing Tactics

Pickleball is a sport that has barreled into the cultural zeitgeist because it is accessible to all. You can grab a paddle, head to a court, make some new friends, and burn a few calories before brunch. But then . . . you miss an easy hit, your ball goes into the net thirteen times in a row, you can't land a serve to save your life, and every time you try to intentionally place a ball somewhere, anywhere, you are reminded that you have zero control over how your paddle participates in this endeavor.

So you start googling, because clearly you are missing something. Clearly there are strategies that can help you overcome this learning curve. All you have to do is master those strategies, and you'll be on the pro circuit in no time. Or, at the very least, you'll be able to hit the damn ball in the general vicinity of where you are aiming. You're not asking for much here.

Hello, Strategy Spiral. Every player goes through it at one point or another, integrating new techniques with the hopefulness of someone who believes a five-minute YouTube tutorial holds the key to greatness.

It starts innocently enough—you add a dink here, a drop there. But eventually, you're overthinking every shot. You're strategizing with your partner mid-game as though huddling up with a clipboard is a common pickleball practice. You dig into blogs, TikToks, and a troubling amount of Reddit threads until your brain is so full of strategy that it short-circuits from too many mental notes every time a ball comes your way. The truth is, the Strategy Spiral is a rite of passage. The only way out is through. With "through" being the point at which a player realizes that simply getting the ball over the net on a consistent basis is the biggest victory of all.

The best skill you'll ever develop during your pickleball journey is the ability to look like you *meant* to do whatever just happened. Especially if whatever just happened resulted in a point for your team, such as:

- **That weird, lingering shot that dribbled over the net into the kitchen? *A delicate dink.***
- **That accidental slam that ricocheted off your partner's forehead? *A brazen poach.***
- **You shuffling around from one side of the court to the other, like a puppy looking for its owner at a dog park? *Just a little advanced switching going on.***

Pickleball players love to throw around terms like "third shot drop," "stacking," and "resetting the point." They sound impressive. They sound tactical. But if you look closely, really closely, you'll notice that most players are just guessing. Loudly. And with confidence.

This chapter is your all-access pass to the beautiful chaos that is pickleball strategy. I'll explore the allegedly "proven" tactics, like dinking and partner positioning, while also celebrating the players who prefer to just hit the ball as hard as they can and hope for the best. You'll learn how to overthink simple shots, confuse your partner with complicated game plans, and make moves as though you know what you are doing. Most important, you'll realize that no matter what strategy you choose, the real secret is this: Always act like it was all part of your plan.

Dink or Dare

The dink is the most common move associated with pickleball: It is a soft, controlled shot that barely clears the net and lands in the kitchen. In the beginning, pickleball was heavy on dinks, which led to epically long dink battles where the ball was gently tapped back and forth for approximately 328 years, with each side waiting for the perfect opportunity to go on the offensive and/or for the other team to just eventually nod off from boredom. These soft, strategic exchanges rewarded players with touch, mental endurance, and knees that could handle squatting for that long.

But in recent years, the game has gotten faster and more aggressive. The rise of better paddles, better athletes, and worse temperaments has seen many players skipping the long dink rallies in favor of hitting the ball as hard as humanly possible. What used to be a friendly tap dance at the net has turned into dodgeball with paddles, a reflex-heavy showdown of speed and sweat.

This shift has created a divide between "bangers" (who hit hard and fast) and "dinkers" (who stick to the soft, controlled game). Many players try to balance both styles, but there's no denying that today's game is louder, faster, and way more frenzied than ever before. Purists see this evolution as a breakdown of skills in favor of brawn, with the fundamentals of the game being pushed aside to make room for those who require grunting in their recreational sports.

DINKERS VS. BANGERS

	Dinking Style (The Soft Game)	Banger Style (The Power Game)
Philosophy	"Patience is a virtue."	"Violence is the answer."
Vibe	Calm, controlled, Mr. Miyagi catching flies with his chopsticks.	Loud, slightly unhinged, over-caffeinated raccoon.
Pros	• Maintains a sense of superiority. • Controls pace and placement. • Psychologically breaks bangers.	• Forces quick reactions. • Wins fast points. • Works out unresolved anger issues via violence against a plastic ball.
Cons	• Takes three years to win one point. • One bad dink can result in a return that punctures your spleen. • Risk of putting everyone to sleep.	• Predictable to skilled opponents. • High probability of the ball banging into the net or into the atmosphere. • May accidentally become known as "That Guy" who is working out his anger issues via violence against a plastic ball.
Common Player Excuse	"I'm just setting up the point."	"My paddle is dead."
Soundtrack	Enya	Death metal

Pickle Strategies

From soft hands to smash attacks, these are the essential strategies (and common screwups) for the different ways people pickle.

✓ For dinkers:

- Dink cross-court (longest distance, more margin for error).
- Dink diagonally from your strong side (whether that be your forehand or backhand, unless your opponent looks nervous, then dink at them).
- Switch up your placements so your opponent can't set up with a lounge chair and a cocktail and still return your shots.

✗ COMMON MISTAKES:

- Forgetting to move your feet. At least give the impression that you are here for cardio.
- Hitting too hard and delivering a perfect opportunity for your opponent to slam the ball back at you.
- Thinking this is more fun than smashing the ball. (It isn't.)

✓ For bangers:

- Drive low and fast toward your opponent's feet to make them cry.
- Target your opponent's paddle shoulder or body to jam their swing, also possibly resulting in tears.
- Hit fast at their weaker player, because this is no place for mercy.
- Keep the tempo high to avoid getting sucked into a dink rally.

✗ COMMON MISTAKES:

- Hitting every ball like a home run derby, all day every day.
- Blasting the ball out of bounds so far it lands in another time zone.
- Getting so addicted to smacking the ball that you forget there are other shots in the game . . . like literally any other shot.

✓ For hybrid players:

- Mix up hard drives and soft drops to keep your opponents guessing.
- Start aggressive to push your opponent back, then suddenly drop it softly into the kitchen when they least expect it.
- Use your drive to set up a dink, and your dink to set up a drive (they'll never know what's coming . . . which tracks, because honestly, neither do you).
- Read your opponents. If they struggle with speed, bring the heat; if they panic on dinks, go soft.

✗ COMMON MISTAKES:

- Overthinking every shot as if you're solving a physics problem in real time.
- Switching strategies too often, leaving both you and your partner befuddled.
- Trying to be too clever, which often results in too many unforced errors.

The Serve and Return: The Opening Act

While many players treat the serve as a glorified "Let's get this party started" ritual, strategy nerds know it's the first opportunity to establish dominance on the pickleball court. We don't just serve and return; we strategize and manipulate. We place and we pace. We . . . well, sometimes we just try to get it over the net, because sometimes that's as strategic as we can muster. We are all out here doing our best.

But if you are aiming to level up your opening act, there are a few simple serve and return tactics that can move you in the direction of at least looking like you know what you are doing. Here is how to serve with style and return with something other than hope and a prayer. Although, let's be honest, it's never a bad idea to throw in hope and a prayer for good measure.

The serve:

- **Make it deep, consistent, and dramatic. Bonus points if you grunt. Everyone respects a grunt.**
- **Aim for your opponent's backhand, if aiming is actually an option.**
- **Add spin (see page 123) if you enjoy watching people suffer, but make sure you really know how to add spin, because if not, you will be the one suffering.**

The return:

- **Also make this deep. Make your opponents stay back, and possibly, hopefully, trip on their own feet.**

- **Hit the ball softly, so it almost floats back to your opponent, giving you time to run up to the net and maybe come up with some pickleball skill in the interim.**

The Third Shot Drop—The Man, the Myth, the Legend

Ah, the legendary third shot drop. Revered by purists, grumbled about by newbies, mastered by . . . like seven people.

What is it? You serve. They return. On the third hit, you gently arc the ball into the kitchen so that it slowly drops just beyond the net, buying yourself time to get up to the kitchen line. That's the idea, anyway. What actually happens: You pop the ball up just high enough for your opponent to promptly crush it into your shoelaces.

Pros preach: "The third shot drop is essential to control the game."

What rec players say: "I figured out the shot, but couldn't quite land the drop."

Key tips:

- **Hit from low to high with a soft arc, as if you have any idea what a soft arc is.**
- **Aim for a bounce in the kitchen; it's important to have goals.**
- **Get ready to mumble a slew of curse words to yourself when it drops on your side of the net instead of the other team's.**

An alternative strategy is to forget the drop and just drive the ball at your opponents' shoelaces. It's not soft, but even if it fails, you at least get a little aggression out.

Reset the Point—Let's Try This Again

Resetting the point is the equivalent of standing in the middle of a group of unruly toddlers, hands up, saying, "Let's tone this down a bit." Except you are one of the toddlers, and you are really close to throwing a temper tantrum because you are losing this point.

When a rally gets out of control–balls flying, bodies flailing–it's usually a sign that your team is struggling. Your only hope is to slow the game down and force the other team to follow suit. The best way to do this is to answer bangers with soft, controlled shots back to the kitchen, the universal sign that Mom is not going to put up with this tomfoolery any longer because someone is going to get hurt (in this case, your pride is most at risk for injury).

The hope is that this soft shot resets the tempo of the point and buys your team a second to regain some footing. It's not flashy. It's not aggressive. But it's the move that separates players who survive chaos from those who collapse in it. Just remember: The goal isn't to win the point, it's to stop losing it–which is the strategy some of us have for every single point, ahem.

Targeting—The Art of Passive-Aggressive Warfare

Let's talk about what you're not supposed to admit you do: targeting the weaker player.

Yes, it's unsportsmanlike.

Yes, it's brutal.

Yes, it's deeply satisfying.

Signs you're being targeted:

- Every ball is hit to you. Every. Single. One.
- Your partner is sunbathing on their side of the court. DoorDash has just delivered them a smoothie.
- Your opponents share a knowing nod after each successful targeting of your weak backhand.

How to fight back:

- Hit dinks at your opponents' feet.
- Sometimes smash a drive into their forehead. Keep things interesting.
- Occasionally hit a winner and shout, "HOW DO YOU LIKE ME NOW?!" You know, to demonstrate how unflappable you are.

Adding Spin—When It's Time to Get Fancy

Right about the time you begin to think you have a handle on pickleball, you'll meet your first spin. There you'll be, finally returning balls, mastering the dinks, feeling pretty cocky. And then out of nowhere, you swing for a ball that spins at you in a way you didn't know a hollow plastic ball could spin, and it bounces off your paddle in a way that seems like a direct insult.

WHAT IS SPIN?

Spin is when you add rotation to the ball, causing it to curve, drop, or bounce in unexpected ways. There's topspin (ball dives downward), backspin (ball floats and stays low), and sidespin (ball curves sideways as if it's looking for a new place to live).

At some point in every young pickleballer's life, they will experiment with spin. For the lucky few, this experiment will add just the right flair to their game. For everyone else, it will result in them out on the court, their "concentration tongue" sticking awkwardly out of the side of their mouth, while the ball misfires off their paddle in directions that defy both physics and common sense. Results may vary.

Why add spin?

- It makes your shots harder to read.
- It messes with your opponent's timing and paddle angle.
- It makes you look like you know what you're doing, even if your tongue sticking out suggests otherwise.

How to add spin (allegedly):

- Topspin (makes the ball dive downward): Brush up on the back of the ball with a quick, snapping motion.
- Backspin (makes the ball float or stay low): Slice under the ball with a soft controlled motion.
- Sidespin (makes the ball curve sideways): Swipe across the ball, side to side.

Common spin player behavior:

- Announces loudly, "Watch this spin," then hits the ball directly into the net.
- So focused on trying to spin every ball that they forget getting the ball over the net is really the biggest goal of the game.
- Exclaims, "Whoa, that was cool!" when a spin comes off their paddle unintentionally.

Adding spin to your pickleball game is the ultimate announcement that you've arrived on the scene as a player who is here to dominate. Or, when the spins go sideways (unintentionally), it's a pretty solid way to announce you have no control over what will be coming from your side of the court. Either way, the opponent is on alert, so not all is lost.

Court Setup Strategies for Partners

Pickleball is most often played as a team sport, which means you should probably think about how to strategize with your partner before you hit the court. How the two of you stand, move, panic, or blame each other can make or break your dreams of pickleball domination and/or survival. Some formations are strategic. Others are accidental. A few are deeply chaotic but weirdly effective. Below are the most common court setups, with a few added in to really level up the shock and awe opportunities on your opponents.

TRADITIONAL FORMATION (SIDE-BY-SIDE)

Each player covers their half of the court, theoretically. This is the most common and straightforward setup, allowing both partners to share the court evenly, also theoretically. It works great when both players trust each other to handle their side and communicate about shots down the middle. It works less great when both players freeze and watch the ball fly through the middle, untouched.

STACKING (SYNCHRONIZED SHUFFLE)

You aren't glued to one side forever; players can switch during play as much as they like. Pickleball is chill like that. The only real rule is that the correct person serves from the correct side. After that, you and your partner can do a full tango around the court if you want.

Which brings us to stacking, where both players start on the same side before the serve and then move into preferred positions once play begins. It's handy when one player has a stronger forehand or backhand. No word from headquarters on what to do if neither partner actually has a strong side.

SWITCHING (TOP-SECRET SHUFFLE)

Switching is just like stacking, but with the element of surprise. While stacking politely announces your intentions before the serve, switching happens mid-rally with no warning—ideally surprising your opponents and, let's be honest, sometimes surprising yourselves. When it works, you look like tactical geniuses. When it doesn't, you might end up running into each other and flopping to the ground like a Looney Tunes cartoon.

ONE UP, ONE BACK (SIDE-EYE FORMATION)

A classic newbie strategy, this formation has one player racing to the kitchen line, while the other remains committed to the baseline. In theory, this court setup covers different areas of the court, but in execution, it leaves a huge vulnerability in the middle of the court. A reality that will delight your opponents and unravel your partnership. You'll spend the match shouting "Up! Back! No, not there! I thought you were covering there!" until one of you gives up and the other pretends you are still working out the kinks in this setup.

POACHING (BALL HOG BALLET)

Poaching isn't so much a strategy as an insult in action. It occurs when one partner lunges across the court to steal every shot that wasn't technically theirs. This strategy can confuse opponents, which can be an advantage. It can also piss off the partner, which is a less productive outcome for the team.

Some players poach because they have quick reflexes and a killer instinct. Others do it because they believe they are the only player on the team qualified to manage any and all returns. An occasional poach can appear heroic, but repeated poaching can look like the beginning of an inevitably loud postgame huddle.

KID 'N PLAY (HOUSE PARTY SWITCH UP)*

Named after the iconic 1990s hip-hop duo, this strategy takes teamwork to a very coordinated level. Instead of a standard switch, partners meet in the middle, lock feet as if they are in a throwback dance-off, and spin to their new positions on the court. It is wildly unnecessary, is completely ridiculous, and will leave opponents frozen in disbelief and utter awe. This provides the perfect opportunity to drop a perfectly placed shot that the other team will be too dumbfounded to return.

ZOMBIE APOCALYPSE (SLOW MARCH TO VICTORY)*

In this strategy, both players move toward the kitchen with the slow methodical shuffling of zombies. No rush, no sudden movements, no blinking. It starts out as a joke, but the laughter fades when it becomes clear that zombies never stop. By the time the laughter dies, the zombies are at the net . . . and it's already too late.

GODZILLA (TOTAL PANIC FORMATION)*

This is less of a strategy and more of a full-blown survival mode. Both players run around the court like extras in a monster movie, except they are running toward a little ball instead of away from a giant lizard's foot. There is no communication, no plan—just players chasing, lunging, cussing, and crying. It's utter chaos that burns a shocking number of calories and occasionally even results in an accidental point or two.

"YOURS!" (THE CALL OF THE WILD)*

This strategy involves playing in tandem with your partner . . . until a ball zips down the middle past the two of you. This is when one partner points at said ball and shouts, "Yours!" Timing is key here. The call must come either just after the ball passes or at the exact moment both partners realize neither has made a move for it. This allows the caller to maintain the illusion that they could have taken it but were generously giving their partner the opportunity to shine. Bonus points if the call comes with a dramatic "How could you MISS THAT?" shrug and a head hung in disappointment.

* Not officially sanctioned setups . . . yet.

SIGNS YOU'RE OVER-STRATEGIZING

Pickleball strategy is great in theory. But if any of the following sound familiar, it might be time to take a deep breath, step away from the YouTube tutorials, and just concentrate on nothing more than hitting the ball over the net.

- You've said "let's reset the point" while arguing with your spouse.
- You analyze each loss like it's game film for the Super Bowl.
- You've practiced footwork in the grocery store produce section.
- You find yourself examining how people are stacking . . . in line at Costco.
- You bring a clipboard to open play. With diagrams.
- You've started practicing your "around the post" shot . . . around your cubicle at work.
- You've tried to "spin" your delivery of the mashed potatoes onto your plate at Thanksgiving dinner.

In the end, strategy isn't about perfection. It's about confidence, quick adjustments, and convincing everyone, yourself included, that your game plan is totally on purpose.

So dink with purpose, spin with style, and target as though you have control over where the ball is going. And, if all else fails, just scream, "Let's GOOOOOOO!" after every point. Who needs instincts when you have intensity?

9

RATE.
REGISTER.
REPEAT.

A Beginner's Guide to Ratings, Tournaments, and the Loss of the "Chill" Pastime

Pickleball is a laid-back game that is friendly and inclusive and . . . did someone mention tournaments? Suddenly there are numbers to obsess over, brackets to conquer, and perhaps a color-coded spreadsheet to create. "Chill" has left the building and has quickly tumbled down the slipperiest of slopes into a place where stats are tracked more closely than bank balances.

The good news is that you'll have a lot of company if you start to slide down this slope. The bad news is everyone swears they're "just here for fun" while showing up looking as if they just stepped out of an Instagram ad for pickleball attire/gear/certifiable obsession.

Let's break down what things look like on the other side of "chill."

The Pickleball Rating System: Myth, Math, or Marketing?

What started as a tool to match players of similar skill levels, the pickleball rating has become a weird little social status symbol in the pickleball world. Ratings tend to "accidentally" come up during warm-ups, are boldly announced at open play, and get casually dropped into postgame conversations like someone reporting their credit score.

"I'm a 3.5."

"We're looking for a 4.0 partner."

"He's at least a 4.5; he could go pro."

The problem? Nobody seems to fully agree on what the ratings mean, how they're determined, or why Barry insists he is a 5.0 when he's currently out on the court in Birkenstocks and a Hawaiian shirt.

Pickleball is all fun and games until a newbie learns about the rating system and immediately becomes obsessed with how they can march their way up the pickleball ratings ladder. Suddenly math has entered the chat, and as everyone knows, math brings nothing but good times to a casual pastime. Why settle for bopping a ball back and forth before heading to brunch when you can download a skill assessment sheet and determine your value on the court and in life via a seemingly arbitrary number?

What exactly is a pickleball rating? Is it earned? Assigned? Is there a panel of judges who hold up cardboard signs with numbers on them if you land an Erne shot? And why does it seem everyone is either inflating or downplaying theirs depending on the circumstance? There are official-sounding acronyms like DUPR (Dynamic Universal Pickleball Rating) and UTPR (USA Pickleball Tournament Player Rating), but also self-ratings that sound about as legitimate as your neighbor's "business opportunity" involving essential oils. So, let's dive into the wonderfully confusing world of pickleball ratings: what they mean, how they are determined (or guessed), and why they matter less than your postgame snack selection.

What Is a Pickleball Rating?

In theory, a pickleball rating is a number, ranging from 1.0 (what is this pickleball you speak of?) to 5.5+ (I'm the best pickler in the world!), used to measure player skill.

In reality, pickleball ratings have become a mix of myth and math, with vibes playing a significant role in the equation. But ultimately, ratings exist to help group players with similar skill levels so matches stay fun and fair. Because no one wants to see a newbie destroyed by "Banger Ben" on a rampage.

SIGNS YOU'RE TAKING YOUR RATING TOO SERIOUSLY

- You've bedazzled your rating on a T-shirt.
- You refer to yourself in the third person by your rating.
- You add your rating to the end of the score call before each serve, "Seven, three, two . . . four point oh!"
- You walk around with a huge sign announcing your rating before each match.

How Do You Rate?

1.0–2.0

"I heard about this new thing called pickleball . . ."

2.5–3.0

"I'm getting the hang of it . . . sort of."

3.5

"I'm . . . dangerously confident."

4.0

"I'm kind of a big deal."

4.5+

"You have probably seen me on your social media feed."

While most rec players casually self-rate (and exaggerate), there are official systems used for tournaments and legitimacy.

DUPR (Dynamic Universal Pickleball Rating): This is a global rating system that calculates a player's skill level on a scale from 2.000 to 8.000 (the extra digits mean "extra special"). Players log the results of all games played (rec or tournament), and their ratings are updated in real time. It's a great tool for those looking to get an accurate rating; it's less fun for those who would like to continue believing they are better than they actually are.

UTPR (USA Pickleball Tournament Player Rating): This is USA Pickleball's official rating system, based only on sanctioned tournament results. It's less dynamic and more exclusive because it doesn't care at all about your rec league domination. It updates whenever it feels like it, which makes it a bit of a drama queen.

Self-Rating: Who needs metrics when you have the honor system? Most pickleballers end up self-rating, which is a fancy way of saying they "just kinda go with their gut" when figuring out their own rating. Sure, there are skill-assessment sheets that can be downloaded, videos that can be watched, ratings calculators that can be consulted, but we have postgame cocktails to attend to; we don't have time for legitimate evaluations.

The go-to number in self-rating? 3.5. It's a number that sounds competent without inviting too much scrutiny. It says, "I know what I'm doing, but I don't want the pressure of having an actual strategy and consistency." And everyone knows that low expectations are the key to success in most areas of life, pickleball included.

Why It Matters (Sorta)

Your rating matters when you are registering for tournaments, getting into leagues, or trying to convince a potential partner that you have the emotional fortitude to survive a dink rally. But if you are just out there to have fun, move your body, and make some friends? It doesn't matter a whole lot. It's worth it to care a little bit about ratings, but not so much that you start demanding three references and a detailed data analysis before agreeing to a doubles match.

When to Tournament: Answering the Call of the Wild

At some point in every pickleball journey, a player will hear the seductive call of The Tournament. The call doesn't come out of nowhere—it slowly bubbles to the surface, waiting for just the right time to present itself.

We start out chill, with low expectations and an even lower skill level. But over time, something starts to shift. We start using words like "stacking" and "unforced error" way more than a person should use those words (and way more than our coworkers want to hear us using those words). And maybe we've won just enough games during rec play to convince ourselves that we are destined for pickleball greatness.

That's when it hits: Tournament Fever.

Tournament Fever is an infection that is highly contagious and commonly transmitted through a phrase like "Have you ever thought about entering a tournament? They are really fun."

"Fun," they said.
"Greatness," you heard.

So you take the leap. And the next thing you know, you are studying DUPR ratings, buying electrolyte packets in bulk, and googling how to handle the retired dentist on court four who has a new knee and a wicked topspin. You've bookmarked three local events, you are researching matching dry-fit team shirts, and you order a sweatband that looks like something a pickleball influencer would definitely wear.

Welcome to the wild side. Welcome to . . . The Tournament.

Types of Tourneys

Pickleball tournaments are happening all over the place, with different degrees of organization and intensity. Some have refs, brackets, and real check-in tables, while others have the vibe of an impromptu hangout with a couple of medals from the dollar store.

They are usually held on weekends, and you'll find them listed on sites like PickleballTournaments.com, through local Facebook groups, promoted by rec leagues, or from fellow players. Tournaments usually divide players by age, gender, and skill rating (official or self-proclaimed) and are filled with the drama of March Madness, the confusion of rugby, and the delusion of thinking bangs are ever a good idea. But before I get to any of that, it's important to know what type of tournament you are signing up for. Each format provides ample opportunity for bangs-like regret, so you are in luck with whatever option you choose.

> ***Round Robin*** **Everyone plays everyone. This is a great way to get a solid idea of your skill level and also to potentially lose ten times in one day.**
>
> ***Single/Double Elimination*** **Some tournaments give you one loss before they kick you out. Others allow two losses. In double elimination, you are moved to the "losers' bracket" after your first loss and then must fight your way back to the top. This sounds like a Disney movie, so bring appropriate music to play in the background.**
>
> ***Pool Play to Bracket*** **This format decided it wanted the best of all worlds and includes a round robin in the first round, followed by single or double elimination in the second round. It's perfect for players who enjoy getting their hopes up just enough to make their eventual defeat feel deeply personal.**
>
> ***Compass Draw*** **Everyone plays, and win or lose, they keep playing. Teams get moved into increasingly obscure brackets seemingly until the end of time. This is a great format if your main goal is quantity over dignity.**

SIGNS YOU ARE SUSCEPTIBLE TO TOURNAMENT FEVER

- ***You start tracking your "record."*** Remember when you used to consider three successful serve attempts in a row as the greatest victory of all? Those days are long gone. Now you are mentally (and maybe physically via a color-coded spreadsheet and/or pickleball app) tracking all of your wins and losses as though they will someday be part of an on-screen chyron during one of your televised matches.
- ***You've said, "I'm probably a 3.5" . . . out loud . . . with a straight face.*** Also, you know what DUPR stands for. You make a point to educate non-pickleballers about the rating system as if it's the stock market and great fortune comes to those who can decipher it.
- ***You've "invested" in a "good paddle."*** You could keep playing with your subpar paddle, but you know it's holding you back from the greatness you are capable of. Sure, paying hundreds of dollars for what is essentially a fancy ping-pong paddle might sound insane, but you know that it is an investment in your potential. And who can really put a price on maximizing potential? (Answer: Paddle manufacturers, that's who.)
- ***You've watched full pickleball matches on YouTube.*** We are not talking just highlights or short clips or funny montages. You've watched full matches with commentary and studied them as though they are research for a dissertation.
- ***You practice . . . on purpose.*** Gone are the days of rolling up to the court three minutes before the game, playing said game, and exiting the court until your next match the following week. You've now worked practice days into your schedule. Maybe you've even downloaded a few drills and brought cones (***cones!***) out to the court. This is getting serious.

Who Will You Become at a Tournament?

Tournaments have a way of revealing things about your pickle persona that you didn't even know existed. Who will you become when thrown into the heat of bracket-based competition?

The Overly Hyped Player **You arrive with notes, a warm-up routine, and two backup paddles. You've tracked carbs and hydration for three days. You are promptly eliminated by a senior citizen and her twelve-year-old grandson.**

The "For the Gram" Player **You aren't really out here to win the games; you are out here to win Instagram. You document every second and create a killer reel that makes you look like a pro, even though the only thing you scored was the swag bag.**

The Intense-O-Rama **You thought you were chill and in control. You thought pickleball was just a casual pastime. You are currently on the ground examining whether the ball left a mark on the line. There is a vein popping out of your forehead that you have never noticed.**

The Puddle **You came into the tournament with a smile and a strut. You leave in a heap of tears and sweat.**

The Justifier **You had an off day. The conditions weren't what you expected. Your paddle is in the shop. Any and all excuses are on the table. Your skills, however, are nowhere to be seen.**

THE WORST TOURNAMENT SWAG BAG

Free Stuff You Technically Paid For

- Commemorative tournament T-shirt (with last year's date on it)
- Coupon for a local chiropractor (along with a map to the nearest urgent care)
- Three crushed granola bars (that expired two years ago)
- One can of beer, one off-brand energy drink (choose your hydration wisely)
- A questionable pickle-themed bumper sticker that will most likely get you weird looks in the school pickup line (complete with a cartoon pickle that looks a little too happy)
- The saddest first aid kit ever: one Band-Aid, a dollop-sized tube of sunscreen, and two unlabeled pills in a snack bag (Are they vitamins, ibuprofen, or Skittles? No one knows!)

Ratings and tournaments have a sneaky way of turning a casual hobby into something that feels an awful lot like a competitive sport. One day you are playing pickup with friends, the next you are planning your PTO around out-of-town tournaments. It's a slippery slope from the Tuesday night rec league to a color-coded spreadsheet tracking DUPR brackets and hydration plans.

If that's the slope you want to ride, go for it. Lean into the competition and see where it takes you. Just don't forget what brought you to the court in the first place: the fun, the cardio, the people, and the ridiculousness of lunging for a plastic ball in shorts you shouldn't have worn. Chase the medals and glory, but don't lose the joy—or wear those shorts again.

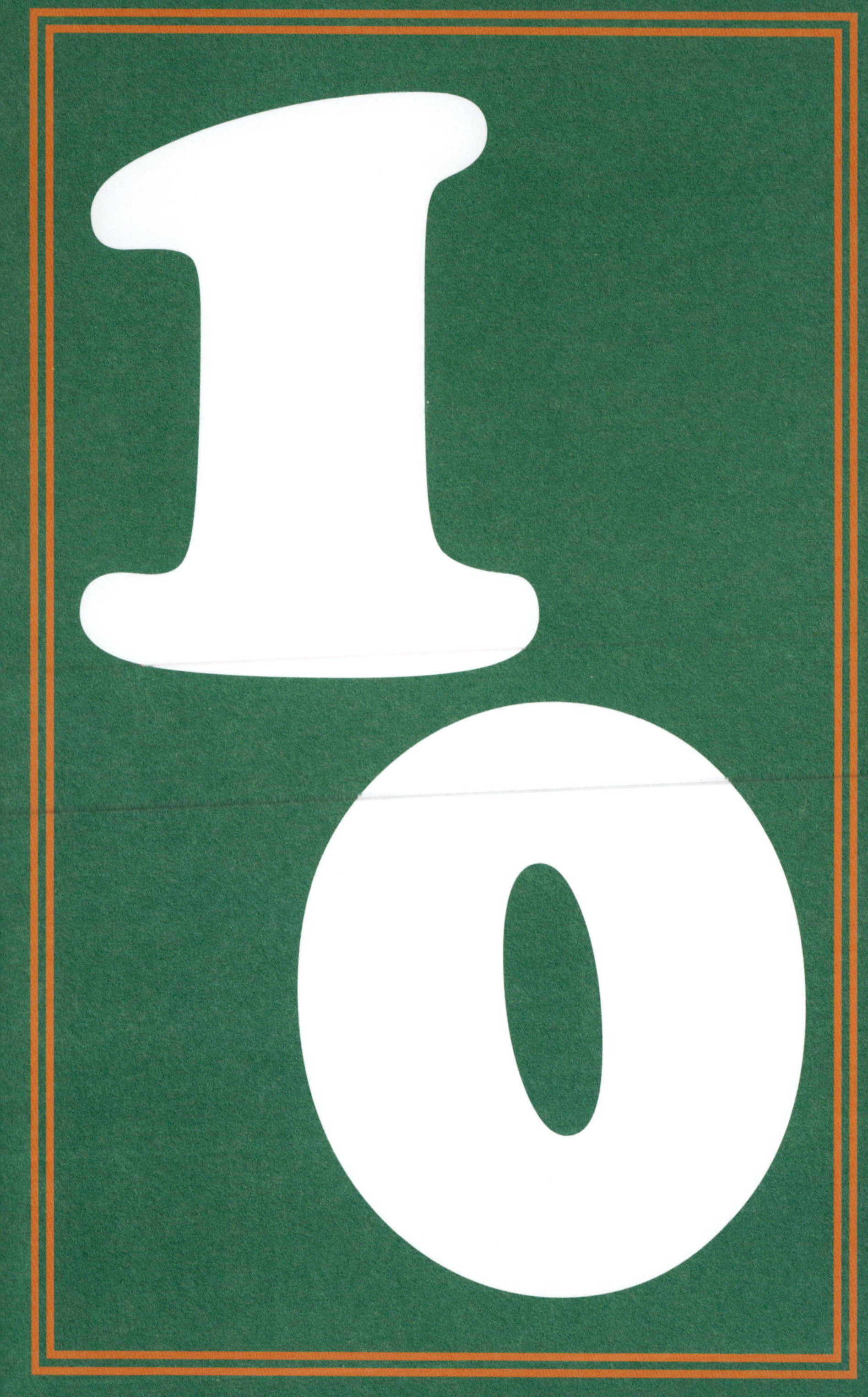

THE PICKLEBALL INJURY HALL OF FAME

Twisted Ankles, Bruised Egos, and Paddle-Induced Trauma

Pickleball likes to bill itself as a harmless little backyard game. Something designed for retirement communities, gym classes, and family barbecues. We're just hitting a little ball back and forth. What could go wrong?

Everything. Everything could go wrong.

Just mention the word "pickleball" around anyone remotely related to any medical field, and you will be met with an involuntary wince similar to the one your kid gives when you peel off a Band-Aid that's been clinging to their leg hair for dear life.

In fact, pickleball's true soundtrack isn't just the pop of the ball or the squeak of shoes on asphalt–it's the chorus of groans, limps, and ice pack rituals that litter the sidelines after every match. Pickleball is an addictive mix of movement, competition, and just enough frenzied excitement to trick people into pushing their bodies a little harder than makes logical sense given their age, athleticism, or general mobility. The result? An ever-growing list of pickleball injuries that range from mildly inconvenient to full-on orthopedic undertaking.

Maybe it's a back strain as you sprint for a drop shot. Maybe it's a rolled ankle after lunging across the kitchen. Or maybe it's something even more uncalled for, like knocking yourself in the face with your own paddle. (I'm not going to sugarcoat it: that's a hard one to shake off.)

Here is the funny part. Everyone thinks injuries happen to other people. The less prepared ones. The ones who don't stretch, or wear bad shoes, or, frankly, are just not as skilled. You, on the other hand, are an *athlete*. You have read *blogs*. You're *different*. Until your body decides that it has had enough of your hubris. Every pickleball

THE UNOFFICIAL PICKLEBALL FIRST AID KIT

- Ice packs (or frozen peas, in a pinch)
- Compression sleeves for every joint you own
- Pain relief cream that smells like questionable recreation choices
- Athletic tape (you won't use it right, but it feels official)
- Backup shoes for your backup shoes
- A whistle to call for help when you can't stand up after a game
- A list of the closest urgent care clinics

player is one overconfident lunge away from realizing they are, in fact, "other people."

And when the body starts complaining, the delusion starts working double time. You promise to stop after one more game, then somehow rattle your joints through four. You ice on the bench, you ignore the fact that you can barely get out of your car when you get home, and you search "quick hamstring rehab" before you even shower. This is not sensible. This is pickleball.

But don't worry, this chapter isn't here to scare you away from the court. It's here to celebrate the wounded warriors. To shine a light on the common (and ridiculous) ways players injure themselves in pursuit of glory (and/or just trying to avoid a face-plant).

So, grab an ice pack, wrap up that swollen ankle, and settle in. This is the chapter where we honor the brave, the overconfident, the injured. Because if you haven't limped off a pickleball court at least once, can you even call yourself a real player?

PADDLE-RELATED INJURIES

When Equipment Goes Rogue

There are a lot of ways to be injured on a pickleball court, but the most insulting has to be when the equipment becomes the culprit in a sneak attack. Sure, paddles look innocent enough, all lightweight and colorful. But in the wrong hands, they become weapons of accidental destruction. They mean well, but all it takes is one overzealous swing, one mistimed reach, or one unfortunate flail, and suddenly you've been attacked by a carbon-cored assassin. Paddle injuries are real, and they're coming for your shins, elbows, and, on very special occasions, your face. Here are the greatest hits (pun intended):

- ***Accidental Partner Smack:*** Usually happens when you both go for a ball, neither calls it, and a paddle hits one or both of you instead of said ball. Poetry in motion, really.
- ***Self-Inflicted Whack:*** You swing, you miss, but your paddle does not give up on its mission to make contact with something. Unfortunately, that something is usually your shin or elbow.
- ***Paddle-to-Face Contact:*** Rare, but unforgettable. Causes include misjudged backhands and teammates with helicopter swings. Sometimes, when the stars align, you can actually hit your own paddle into your own face, which will become the lowlight of your game and the highlight of the night for anyone lucky enough to be a witness.

Possible Pickleball Injuries

HEAD, NECK, AND SHOULDERS

1. ***Concussion*** Can happen as a result of a run-in with the ground, your partner, a paddle. Injury to dignity also included at no extra charge.
2. ***Whiplash*** Happens when you whip your head around to watch a ball go whizzing down the middle past you and your partner.
3. ***Shoulder strain/rotator cuff injury*** Caused by repetitive high-impact movement. Most commonly caused by overly ambitious smashes, missile launch serves, and those leaping saves (where you imagine yourself as an elegant gazelle, but in reality look more like a drunk reindeer).
4. ***Battered ego*** The emotional damage sustained from any number of flubs one can experience when overconfidence meets the reality of your performance abilities.

ARMS, ELBOWS, AND WRISTS

5. ***Tennis/golfer's elbow*** So many names for the same thing: You are playing a sport too much, too often, and your body has had enough of it.
6. ***Hyperextended celebration fist*** One must rein in the exuberance, or risk a celebration-related injury.
7. ***Wrist sprain/strain*** When gravity takes over, it's your poor wrists that are the last line of defense before impact. And they usually aren't quite up for the task of supporting your entire body weight.

8. ***Bone fractures*** Because the court is hard and bones don't always bounce. Tripping, slipping, or landing wrong can result in injuries that are way beyond the healing power of ibuprofen.

BACK AND CORE

9. ***Lower back strain/spasms*** Lunging for that low ball felt majestic until you tried to stand up again.
10. ***Oblique strain*** You'd spent your entire life blissfully unaware that you even had oblique muscles, only to make the most unfortunate of introductions shortly after twisting your body in a way it was never intended to twist.
11. ***Pulled dignity muscle*** When your body says no, but your pride says, "I got this."

HIP AND GROIN

12. ***Hip flexor strain*** Your hips don't lie, and they also aren't a huge fan of the explosive lunges you've added to your regularly scheduled laziness.
13. ***Groin pull*** You "go big" as if you're clearing hurdles in the Olympics. Your inner thigh very politely reminds you it's time to "go home."

LEGS AND KNEES

14. ***Hamstring strain/pull*** You sprinted as though you were still in high school. The pop you just heard from your hamstrings would like to remind you . . . you are not.
15. ***Knee pain*** If you're lucky, you will get away with some minor knee aches and maybe some scrapes and bruises. Odds are that luck will run out.

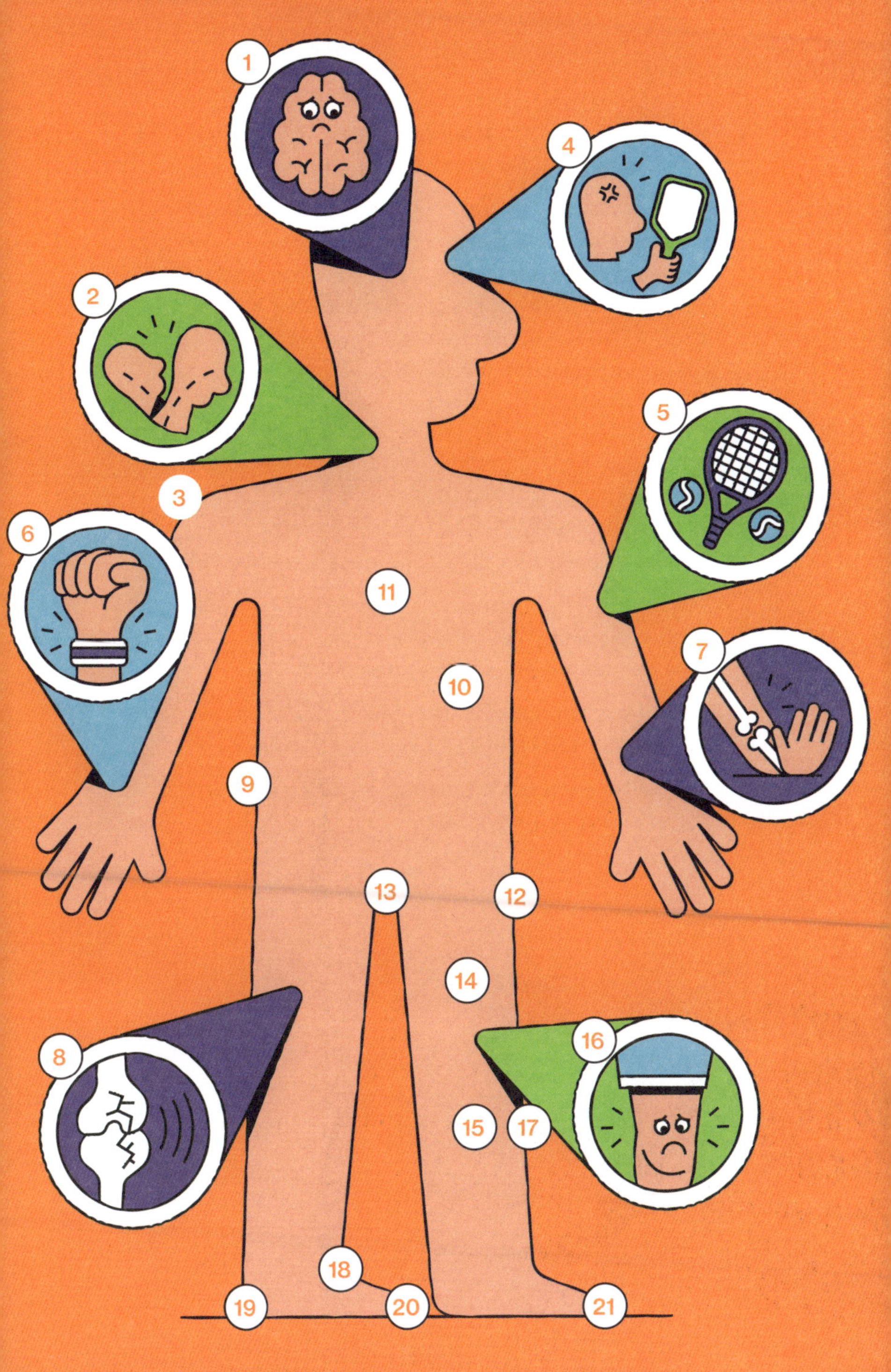
1
4
2
5
3
6
11
7
10
9
13
12
14
8
16
15
17
18
19
20
21

16. *Meniscus tear* A small piece of cartilage standing between you and six weeks of physical therapy.

17. *ACL/MCL strains or tears* The knee's way of saying, "We are officially maxed out on fun here." These are serious injuries that usually show up when different parts of your body don't get the memo on what direction everyone else is headed. Dramatic saves, awkward landings, and quick direction changes can lead to the waiting room instead of the highlight reel.

ANKLES AND FEET

18. *Ankle sprain/twist* One of the first injuries many pickleballers experience, shortly before investing in proper footwear.

19. *Plantar fasciitis (heel pain)* Because your arch support gave up somewhere around game three.

20. *Foot blisters* A reminder that brand-new shoes might not love you back right away.

21. *Toe bruise* From when you tripped over your own feet thirteen times in one game.

FAMOUS LAST WORDS

"I think I felt something pop."

"I don't need to warm up,
I'm already loose."

"The strain will work itself out."

"Maybe I should've stretched."

"I'm gonna take it easy this game."

"I think I can reach that."

"Check back in a few minutes;
I'm sure I'll be able to move then."

THE WIND, THE SUN, THE PADDLE

And Other Totally Valid Excuses for Losing

Once you've tackled the strategies, equipment, and gear needed for pickleball success, it is equally important to ready a mountain of excuses to explain away your inevitable pickleball failures. Because what is friendly competition if not a playground of delusions, deflections, and damage control?

Excuses are the bedrock of all recreational sports, and pickleball is no different. Our egos demand that we leave the court with a rock-solid excuse, one that makes it crystal clear our loss had nothing to do with our skill level, and everything to do with forces completely outside of our control. Obviously.

Blaming external factors is practically a sport within the sport. Was it the wind? The sun? Your paddle? The fact that your partner was "off their game"? Yes. It was all those things. How could anyone be expected to prevail under such circumstances? They couldn't. Obviously.

Excuses are more than postgame chatter; they are performance art mixed with just enough delusion and fake science to make everyone nod along as if you might be on to something. They allow us to rewrite the story in real time, turning embarrassing defeats into epic tales of perseverance against unbeatable odds. Think *Rudy, Rocky* (first movie), and *Cool Runnings.* All winners in our hearts, if not so much on the scoreboard.

This chapter is your guide to the greatest hits of pickleball excuse-making. Study them, memorize them, and use them freely out there on the courts. Because when the score doesn't go your way (and this will happen a lot), you'll need to be ready with an excuse so convincing even your opponents might question whether they deserved to win at all.

The Wind

Let's start with the MVP of excuses: the wind. Wind is a great excuse because it can come and go, shift on a dime, and everyone knows that pickleballs are basically designed to be held hostage by a light breeze.

Go-to excuses:

"Oh, man, the wind carried it wide!"

"Every time I go to serve, here comes the wind!"

"You're so lucky the wind is at your back!"

Some opponents may point out that they are playing in the same wind, but this is where you sidestep a little and point out the unpredictability of nature's fan. Stay strong and loud—this is your reputation on the line.

The Sun

Ah, the blinding fireball in the sky that is on a constant mission to ruin your pickleball game. While the sun technically shines on all players, you have clearly been targeted by the solar flare.

Go-to excuses:

"I couldn't see it. The sun was right there."

"I forgot my good sunglasses at home!"

"Who scheduled this game at high noon?!"

For maximum effect, squint dramatically at the sky after every missed shot, shielding your eyes with your paddle as if you've just emerged from an underground bunker and are seeing sun for the first time in a decade.

The Paddle

When in doubt, blame the equipment. How can you be expected to perform when you have such a subpar paddle to work with?

Go-to excuses:

"This paddle has no sweet spot."

"I just switched paddles–not quite used to it yet."

"This paddle has the wrong kind of core composition for this humidity."

Bonus points if you stare at the paddle, shake your head in disappointment, and say something like, "Yeah, I'm going to have to return this."

The Ball

How can one be expected to play pickleball when the *ball* is not bouncing right? You've seen a pitcher inspect and return a few baseballs before landing on the perfect one to throw, right? There's no reason you can't do the same in pickleball. Except you should do it *after* you've lost the point, for dramatic flair.

Go-to excuses:

Inspecting the ball an inch from your eye: "Oh, man, yeah, just what I thought . . . this ball is cracked. Barely visible, but definitely there. Thought I heard it bounce weird. That explains a lot."

"These are indoor balls, and we are outside."

"These aren't the brand I'm used to playing with."

Maybe even switch balls mid-game for maximum effect and let it be known that you are not happy with the quality of the ball on this court. (The quality of your play is not up for discussion at this time.)

The Court

When all else fails, blame the ground.

Go-to excuses:

"This court feels too slick."

"I think there's a slight slope—do you feel that?"

"The lines are totally faded; I can't even tell where the court ends."

Every tiny pebble or patch of moisture is open for inspection and blame, because how are you expected to play under these conditions?

Physical Limitations (Real or Imagined)

Nothing legitimizes a loss faster than casually mentioning an unverified medical condition. For extra points, be sure to foreshadow this condition throughout gameplay with a grimace here and a limp there. Add in a few torso twists or knee stretches between points to let everyone know you are really struggling with something out here.

Go-to excuses:

"Oh, man, I reached for the ball and *pop*, there goes my back again. I had to take it slow after that."

"My doctor told me I should sit out for a couple more weeks, but I wanted to get moving again. Definitely not at my normal pace, though."

"I didn't hydrate enough this morning."

Mention a joint or muscle with just enough specificity to sound credible, but not so specific that anyone can fact-check you. When pushed, just say you are waiting to hear back from your physical therapist for a specific rehab plan.

Partner Problems

The best part about playing doubles is that there is always another person on your side of the net who could theoretically be responsible for your team's failure. And since you are clearly not

THE OFFICIAL PICKLEBALL EXCUSE GENERATOR

Blame Target	Dramatic Add-On
The Wind	". . . was against me the whole time."
The Sun	". . . completely threw off my rhythm."
The Paddle	". . . was basically working for the other team."
The Ball	". . . was just not what I'm used to."
The Court	". . . isn't regulation. I'm gonna need to look it up."
My Back	". . . messed with my energy today."
My Partner	". . . just wasn't right. I felt it in my core."
The Universe	". . . cost me at least four points, maybe five."

Example Result

"**The wind** . . . was against me the whole time."

"**My back** . . . isn't regulation, I'm gonna need to look it up."

responsible for anything resembling failure, the math has made it pretty clear who is at fault. You don't have to say it *outright,* but you can definitely paint a pretty obvious picture.

Go-to excuses:

"We're still working on our communication."

"We haven't played together much."

"I'm used to playing on the left side, but I had to switch."

If they make a mistake? Give a supportive "All good, we'll get the next one." But make sure you make eye contact with a nearby spectator to confirm that *clearly* you are carrying this team.

Rule Confusion

No one really has any idea what is going on with regard to ever-changing pickleball rules. And it is well-known that rules have a tendency to vary based on where the game is being played. Use this discrepancy in your favor and lean into the confusion when it suits your narrative.

Go-to excuses:

"Oh, my bad, that's not how we play at my home court."

"Wasn't that a fault?"

"Oh, I'm used to rally scoring." (Even if you aren't.)

It doesn't matter if the rule you are referencing has nothing to do with what just happened on the court. The goal is to keep people off-balance and ready to accept that your defeat comes with an asterisk.

The Universe

The wind, your paddle, and your partner are all real things that can be fact-checked in real time. So, when all those facts aren't in your favor, you gotta go with the big guns: the universe itself. Sure, the wind died down, and the sun was behind the clouds, but you know what was off? The vibes. And there is nothing that can be done to overcome bad vibes.

Go-to excuses:

"Mercury is in retrograde."

"I should have saged my paddle."

"My tarot card reader told me this was going to happen."

Energy is untouchable and undeniable. Game. Set. Excuse.

The Ultimate Excuse: "I Was Just Having Fun"

When all else fails, go with the tried-and-true excuse of every person who has ever been overly invested in rec sports, only to see themselves fail spectacularly. Shrug and say, "Oh, yeah, I wasn't really trying. Just out here burning some calories and having some fun. Going about sixty percent speed, you know. Keepin' it light."

Who can argue with that level of unbothered? No one. Their victory means nothing because you were just out here to catch some rays and some high fives. What score? You can't even remember what the score was. Who even cares? *Not you.* That's who.

LOSE-O-METER

How Different Players Handle Defeat

- ***The Graceful Exiter:*** Smiles, says, "Good game," taps paddles at the net, and walks off without incident.
- ***The Self-Deprecating Shrugger:*** Laughs it off, blames themself, and pretends they're totally fine with the loss. Totally fine. Immediately goes home and spends 3.5 hours watching YouTube tutorials.
- ***The Excuse Machine:*** Clearly this loss was not their fault. There were so many factors that played into things not going their way, it's probably easier to just call this one a draw and try again another day, when the conditions are fair for everyone. Clearly.
- ***The Silent Sulker:*** Zero eye contact following the last point. Packs up their gear in silence. Wants nothing to do with postgame banter or talk of grabbing a beer. There is no joy in defeat, only crippling silence and endless reflection.
- ***The Epic Meltdown:*** Paddle and profanity are thrown with abandon. Followed by a dramatic exit stage right that includes listing all injustices that were committed against them during this match and possibly dating back to childhood. Announces they are done with the game, even though everyone knows the show will have a repeat performance the very next day.

GRAND FINALE

The Beginning of the Obsession

From the kitchen to the Cry Zone, you've made it to the end of this glorious, slightly unhinged journey through the world of pickleball. You've learned the jargon, you've questioned the fashion, and you might even finally be able to call the score without panicking (most of the time).

And now there is just one more step for you to take. This chapter isn't about learning. It's about becoming. Because if you are doing it right, pickleball is not just a sport, it's a lifestyle. A full-body transformation that starts with a borrowed paddle and ends with, well, probably a visit to the podiatrist. But just beyond the paddle cores, kitchen rules, and wind excuses lies the pinnacle of pickle: The Obsession.

The moment this "fun" little rec sport becomes your entire identity. The moment you start skipping family functions to play "just one more," you book vacations based on court proximity, and you keep backup paddles in your trunk . . . just in case.

You have arrived, and there is no going back. You are one of the few, the proud, the pickled. You've earned the bruises, the friends, and the weird tan lines. Now it's time to take it to the next level. Welcome to The Obsession. Let's go big.

Cue the Delusion

Sure, you've got the basics of pickleball down: You know how to serve, you know how to stack, you've been known to throw in an occasional spin. That's all well and good. But in order to fully cross over into obsessed territory, you are going to need one more key ingredient in your pickle punch. And that ingredient is a very healthy dose of delusion.

There can be no wavering on this. You must delude yourself into fully believing that you are *thiiiiiiiis* close to going pro. There is a 5.0 player lurking inside of you, just waiting to be unleashed upon the world. This is your mantra, this is your drive, this is your destiny. All you need are a few more tournaments under your belt . . . and maybe a shoulder brace . . . and then . . . it's on.

The Court Is Where You Reside, Both Emotionally and Spiritually

You used to play once a week. Wasn't that cute?

Now, your phone automatically suggests directions to nearby pickleball courts any time you leave the house. Because that's where you always end up. Your calendar is a littered mess of open play, league nights, practice times, and private lessons.

You've memorized the details of different courts like other people recall the layouts of their childhood homes. You know which net leans slightly left, which surface has an unforgiving glare, and which sides catch the crosswind. You hold grudges against certain courts that betrayed you during important matches. These are not just courts anymore. They are battlefields. They are sanctuaries. They are home.

You Must Spread the Word

The most important step in any irrational obsession is the evolution into full-on proselytization.

It is not enough for you to embrace the Passion of the Pickle. You must also share that passion with all who will listen (or all who can't figure out how to extricate themselves from a conversation with you).

Every new person you meet is a potential doubles partner; every casual "How's it going?" is an opportunity to explain court positioning; every group chat is in need of at least five pickleball-themed memes a day. You can't help it. You can't stop, won't stop.

Your friends? Confused and a little concerned. Your coworkers? U-turning away from you in the hallway while avoiding eye contact. Your chiropractor? Very rich. Your soul? Fulfilled.

You are not just a player—you are a believer. And you have two paddles and a performance visor in your trunk, just waiting for your next convert.

WHERE TO PICKLE

Epic Playgrounds for Hardcore Picklers

Pickleball's popularity has officially busted out of local rec centers and hit the road for a worldwide adventure tour. Why settle for simple weeknight matches when you can paddle away on a floating court in the Adriatic Sea or dink thirty stories above Manhattan with the New York City skyline in the background? We're talking women's-only mountain retreats where we get in touch with our feelings and our third shot drop; frozen lake showdowns in Canada, where you swap court shoes for ice skates and pray your ankles are up for the challenge; cruise ship tournaments that take place between buffet visits and unnecessary dance parties by the pool. From deserts to rooftops, beaches to boats, today's pickleball options are only limited by how much vacation time you have and how many paddles you can cram into your carry-on. Because pickleball isn't just growing—it's globetrotting like it has a bucket list and a trust fund.

When you are ready to level up your pickleball life, there are courts waiting for you in all corners of the world, so grab your paddle and some sensible shoes, and start cashing in those airline miles.

Exotic places to pickle:

- Inflatable courts tethered to yachts or designed for lakes, pools, and bays (finally, a soft landing for your ill-advised ATP attempt)
- Cruise ships and riverboats (perhaps the waves will give you an unintentional but highly effective spin)
- Rooftops in busy cities (when you want to really level up your out-of-bounds hits)
- Themed entertainment venues (think pickle and party)
- Beachside resorts (who needs electrolytes when you have pineapple drinks?)
- Luxury all-inclusive pickleball vacations (all you can eat, drink, and dink)
- Wellness and spa retreats (get a little zen following your on-court, profanity-laced tirade against your own backhand)
- On ice, in skates (this sounds cold and unnecessary; let's go back to the beach)

Places to pickle soon enough:

- Pickleball Space Station Invitational (you just know a billionaire is trying to figure out how to make this happen)
- Mount Everest Base Camp Open (altitude training meets paddle clashing)
- Subway Station Pickleball League (strategically place shots around rats and angry commuters)
- Area 51 Pickleball Complex (glow-in-the-dark balls, government agents in aviator sunglasses, unidentified flying objects occasionally coming into contact with your shot)
- Your neighborhood court (hey, everything old is new again!)

"If You Build It . . . the HOA May Come"

At some point in the progression of every obsession, a pickleball player thinks, wishes even, "What if I just built my own court?"

It starts out simple enough. A little googling here, a tape measure there. Before long, you have created a fifteen-slide PowerPoint presentation for your spouse titled "The Resale Value of Homes with Pickleball Courts."

Next thing you know, you've watched 278 YouTube videos of backyard DIY court builds and are designing Evites to a Saturday morning drop-in league in your cul-de-sac. You are now the mayor of Pickleballville. Congratulations.

Possible home court locations:

- The backyard (who needs grass, anyway?)
- The driveway (with chalk lines that come and go with the seasons)
- The living room (cost savings from not having to furnish!)
- The dog run (sorry, Fido)
- The garage (cars can survive in the elements just fine)
- The street (a neighborhood that plays together . . . doesn't alert the HOA together)

How to Obsess— A Final Checklist

Here is everything you need to take a jumping leap over the line between casual player to full-court pickleball zealot.

Fashion:

- ✔ "Just for pickleball" socks that are indistinguishable from regular socks (but you know the difference)
- ✔ At least three performance shirts that feature unnecessary and moderately offensive pickle puns
- ✔ Performance sunglasses that cost more than your car payment
- ✔ At least two sweatbands you don't need . . . but emotionally require

Gear:

- ✔ Four custom paddles, each with its own matching paddle cover
- ✔ A court bag large enough to house gear, snacks, backup gear, and possibly an automatic ball launcher
- ✔ A water bottle marked with 739 stickers, each carefully selected and placed as a representation of you as a person and a player
- ✔ Indoor *and* outdoor balls, because you're a civilized athlete now
- ✔ Shoes with lateral support, arch cushioning, and a five-minute promo reel on social media

Court life:

- ✔ Weather apps bookmarked just for wind speed on outdoor courts
- ✔ A mental map of every local court that includes restrooms, shaded benches, and electrical outlets for your ball machine
- ✔ A detailed and highly scientific ranking of all the pickleball partners you've played with
- ✔ A go-to excuse for every missed shot, ideally delivered with the passion of a closing argument to the Supreme Court
- ✔ A pre- and post-play ritual that is three times as long as the actual matches

Personal:

- ✔ A group chat that's 90% pickleball memes and 10% actual scheduling
- ✔ A long list of non-pickleball family and friends whom you have blown off in favor of feeding your pickle passion
- ✔ Working knowledge of paddle core technology and very little knowledge of current events
- ✔ One recurring injury you have considered making the basis of your memoir
- ✔ A pretty major delusion that you could actually go pro if you *just had more time to practice*

Game. Set. Icy Hot.

So here we are, at the end of this very official, extremely academic exploration of all that is pickleball. If you've made it this far, you are either deeply committed to the sport or are currently immobilized by a postgame injury and are unable to leave the couch for the foreseeable future. In fact, you may actually be both of those things.

However you stumbled into pickleball, and this book, I'm glad you are here. I hope this book reminded you that there's magic in the mayhem, lessons in the learning curve, and comedy literally everywhere you look on the court.

Because pickleball, for all its quirks, is more than just dinks and drama. It's a gateway to community, endorphins, and so many different amazing (if questionable) fashion choices. It's where strangers become teammates, sore muscles become bragging rights, and every game is an opportunity to push the limits of your comfort zone and your cartilage. Concurrently.

Whether you're dreaming of medals or just hoping to make it through a match without pulling five to twelve muscles, remember: This sport is not really about winning. It's about camaraderie, blaming the wind, and fully committing to the idea that you are one magic paddle (and probably a couple of knee braces) away from a 5.0 rating.

So here's to the questionable line calls and the unlikely friendships that are born from shared joint pain. To the frustrations of trying something new and the rare moments when your inner champion shows up just long enough to pull off a feat of athletic wonder on the court. To the menacing backhands, airtight excuses, and legendary postgame snacks.

I'll see you out on the court. You bring the ibuprofen, and I'll bring the unwarranted confidence. And we can both pretend we have an actual strategy for victory.

Glossary

ATP (Around the Post): A shot hit around the net post, not over it.

Backspin (or Slice): A reverse spin that makes the ball float or stay low.

Ball Hog: A partner who tries to hit every ball, regardless of whether it's theirs.

Banger: A player who hits everything hard and calls it "strategy."

Baseline: The back boundary line of the court.

Big Bird: An unofficial formation where one partner climbs on the other's shoulders. Technically illegal. Spiritually unstoppable.

Blame Bench: Where partners go to subtly (or not-so-subtly) explain why that last point definitely wasn't their fault.

Bounceinator: The player who bounces the ball 2,548 times before each serve. Is it a tic? Is it intimidation? Is it infuriating? Yes.

Brace Phase: That time in every pickleball journey when joints become unwilling to participate without support of some kind.

Cardio with Consequences: The real name for pickleball. Also a decent band name.

Cauliflower: A player who brings the same unnecessary intensity to pickleball that cauliflower brings to pretending it's bread.

Chili Cheese French Fries: A full-sprint, full-regret lunge for a hopeless shot. Alluring, messy, and instantly regrettable.

Cross-Court: A diagonal shot from one side of the court to the opposite.

Cry Zone: That special place on the court reserved for processing mid-game injuries to the body and/or soul.

Dillball: A shot that is inbounds and has bounced once; a live ball.

Dink: A soft shot that drops just over the net into the kitchen.

Dink Daddy/Paddle Princess: Elite pickleball personas. Dripping in gear, attitude, and personalized Etsy purchases.

Double Bounce Rule: The ball must bounce once on each side following the serve before players can start hitting volleys out of the air.

Drive: A hard, direct shot.

Drop Shot: A soft shot intended to land just over the net into the kitchen.

Emotional Support Paddle: The backup paddle that holds no real purpose except to be ready to rock if the primary paddle is unable to perform.

Erne: An advanced shot hit in the air while jumping outside the sideline near the kitchen.

Fault: A rules violation that ends the rally.

Foot Fault: Stepping into the kitchen on a volley or onto the baseline while serving.

Fully Pickled: Final form of the transition from casual pickleballer to obsession.

Ghost Paddle: That moment when the ball mysteriously passes through your paddle.

Gravity's Playground: The Kitchen. Where your dreams (and your dignity) go to face-plant.

Huddle Upper: Wants a team meeting after every point.

Ice Cream Truck: A rogue plastic ball that rolls forever while you chase it like a kid who hears the distinctive ice cream truck jingle in the distance.

Kermit: A cheerful newbie flailing around the court with reckless joy and zero coordination. May or may not hum a little ditty when serving.

Kitchen (Non-Volley Zone, or NVZ): The seven-foot area by the net where volleying is not allowed.

Kitchen Chicken: A player too scared to enter the kitchen, for fear of foot faulting their way to defeat.

Kitchen Couture: A pickleball ensemble that says, "I may not know how to announce the score, but I certainly know how to announce my fashion sense."

Kitchen Riot: When dinks and feet are all up in the kitchen, a chaos rally with no clear winner.

Lob: A high, arcing shot that aims for the back of the court.

Lob Goblin: A chaotic creature who lives only to lob.

Moaner: Groans, sighs, and mutters ominously throughout the game, leaving everyone else to wonder if the player is in pain or about to cause others pain.

Nasty Nelson: When a server "accidentally on purpose" nails the non-receiving opponent with the ball, earning a point and probably a lot of glares from everyone in the vicinity.

Oscar: The trash-talking player who never moves an inch. Stationary, grumpy, and oddly intimidating.

Paddle Face: The material that is used to cover the surface of a paddle.

Paddle Identity: A complete personality shift caused by purchasing a new paddle.

Pickle: The name of the game. No one really knows why.

Pickleball Divorce: When spouses have loud on-court arguments followed by very quiet rides home.

Pickled: Losing 11–0. Cue "womp womp" music.

Pickler: A person hopelessly addicted to pickleball.

Pivot: Rotating your body and feet (without lifting your anchor foot) to stay balanced and ready to handle any shot.

Poach: Jumping into your partner's territory for a shot.

Reset the Point: A soft, controlled shot used to regain composure and slow down the pace.

Side-Eye Section: Sideline spectators who have zero authority but maximum judgment.

Smash (aka BLAM-O): A powerful shot hit above the head to finish the rally.

Soft Game (Dinking Style): A style of play focused on dinks and touch instead of power and smashes.

Stacking: A doubles strategy where both players start on one side for strategic positioning.

Strategy Spiral: The slippery slope from "just having fun" to watching YouTube tutorials for the entirety of your lunch break every day.

Targeting: Polite name for hitting every ball to the weaker player until they cry.

Third Shot Drop: A soft, strategic third shot that is played after the serve and return and lands in the kitchen, allowing the serving team to move up to the net.

Topspin: Forward spin applied to the ball to keep it low and controlled.

Transition Zone: The area between the baseline and kitchen where chaos often lives.

Tweener: A shot made between the legs.

Unforced Error: A mistake made on an easy shot when there was absolutely no excuse besides user error.

Volley: Hitting the ball before it bounces.

Wind Excuse: Classic defense against poor performance. Your shot was perfect; nature just pulled it out of bounds. It is an injustice.

"Yours!": Translation: I absolutely do not have it, and now neither do you.

About the Author

Dawn Dais is a freelance writer and designer who has made a career out of poking fun at the "newbie experience." Whether she is tackling pregnancy, parenting, or running, Dawn has been there, stumbled through it, and somehow survived to tell the tale—usually with a healthy dose of sarcasm. Dawn lives in Roseville, California, with her blended family of six humans, four cats, and the occasional raccoon who has figured out the cat door.

Her pickleball journey began, as so many great legends' do, in the trash. One day, while out on a neighborhood stroll, Dawn noticed a box of discarded items on the sidewalk. Poking out of the box—like an invitation, like an answer—was a paddle boldly stamped *The Best Paddle.* She picked it up, and with it, her destiny. Later she learned the paddle brand had been cofounded by Jamie Foxx, a detail that makes zero sense and yet cannot be denied.

And so, this book is brought to you by fate, curbside cast-offs, and Jamie Foxx's entrepreneurial spirit. May all your greatest journeys be equally confounding and rewarding.

Find Dawn online at dawndais.com.

ABOUT THE ILLUSTRATOR

Tim Alexander is a commercial vector illustrator based in Brighton, United Kingdom, and is represented worldwide by Making Pictures. His approach to image making is focused on creative problem-solving by breaking down concepts to reassemble them into clean, sharp illustrations with a focus on geometric shapes and fun, playful energy. Select clients include *The New York Times,* Bloomberg, and *The Wall Street Journal.*

Index

TEN SPEED PRESS
An imprint of the Crown Publishing Group
A division of Penguin Random House LLC
1745 Broadway
New York, NY 10019
tenspeed.com
penguinrandomhouse.com

A Ten Speed Press Trade Paperback Original

Typefaces: Bitstream's Cooper, Commerical Type's Neue Haas Grotesk, and Hoodzpah's Redondo Ave

Paper Texture by somchaip/Adobe Stock, page 50 (left) by 4x6/Getty Images, page 50 (right) by ViDI Studio/Shutterstock, page 51 (left) by Siri Stafford/Getty Images, page 51 (right) by Cultura Creative/Getty Images, page 52 (left) by Ljupco Smokovski/Shutterstock, page 52 (right) by gpointstudio/Deposit Photos, page 53 (left) by 4x6/Getty Images, page 53 (right) by Roman Samborskyi/Shutterstock, page 70 by Experienced Skins/Getty Images

Library of Congress Cataloging-in-Publication Data is on file with the publisher.

ISBN 978-0-593-83961-4
Ebook ISBN 978-0-593-83962-1

Editor: Julie Bennett
Production editor: Abby Oladipo
Designer: Isabelle Gioffredi
Art director: Emma Campion
Production designers: Mari Gill, Faith Hague, and Mara Gendell
Production: Jessica Heim
Copy editor: Ethan Campbell
Proofreaders: Jacob Sammon and Sarah Rutledge
Publicist: Soren Eversoll
Marketer: Joey Lozada

Manufactured in China

10 9 8 7 6 5 4 3 2 1

The authorized representative in the EU for product safety and compliance is Penguin Random House Ireland, Morrison Chambers, 32 Nassau Street, Dublin D02 YH68, Ireland, https://eu-contact.penguin.ie.